New Songs of Rejoicing

David P. Schaap, editor

Selah Publishing Co.

Acknowledgments

The poets and composers whose work is the substance of this collection are to be thanked for their creativity and contribution to congregational song. Their work gives us hope, joy, and understanding.

I am indebted to Robert Schreur for his numerous readings of and valuable contributions to *New Songs of Rejoicing*. The staff of Selah Publishing Co. has done much work to bring this collection into existence, and I express my thanks to Linda Grapel, Theresa LaGattuta-Bruno, Susan Hermance, Sarah Bonsteel, and especially Virginia Lee Ellis.

I would like to acknowledge Henry Admiraal for his work on the scriptural index and Mary Louise VanDyke who supplied answers to make the credits more accurate. Additionally, I would like to thank those whose names follow who have helped in the growth of Selah as a publisher of church music and congregational song by their support and encouragement: Emily Brink, Allen Freeman, Percival W. Gazlay II, Joan and Nicholas Huizenga, Susan Huizenga, Elsa and Abigail Katzell, Richard Kollath, Iteke Prins, Edgar R. Schaap, Rose Schaap, W. Thomas Smith, Dorothy and Dale VanHamersveld, Janet Vincent-Scaringe, and John Worst have helped in ways too numerous to mention. My thanks to all of them.

David P. Schaap

 Printed on recycled and acid-free paper

Copyright © 1994, Selah Publishing Co., Inc., Kingston, N.Y.

All rights reserved.

All pieces in this collection are under copyright protection of the copyright holder listed with each hymn. Permission must be obtained from the copyright holder to reproduce—in any form or by any means, electronic, mechanical, photocopying, or otherwise—what is included in this book. The address of companies that hold copyrights are listed in the back of the book.

Every effort has been made to trace the owner or holder of each copyright. If any rights have been inadvertently infringed upon, the publisher asks that the omission be excused and agrees to make the necessary corrections in subsequent printings.

Typeset and printed in the United States of America.

First edition
2 3 4 5 6 7 8 9 10 00 99 98 97 96 95 94

ISBN 0-9622553-9-4

Contents

Acknowledgments .... [2]
Introduction .... [4]
Hymns for the Church Year
    Advent 1
    Christmas 8
    Epiphany and Life of Christ 16
    Lent 25
    Easter 35
    Ascension and Reign 38
    Pentecost and the Holy Spirit 40
Biblical Songs
    Psalm settings 43
    Settings of Scripture 60
Hymns for the Church in the World
    Creation and Providence 76
    Redemption 90
    Church and Mission 95
    Christian Life 100
    Mystery of God 126
    New Heaven and Earth 133
    Society 136
Hymns for the Church at Worship
    Opening of Worship 141
    Confession and Forgiveness 145
    Dedication and Offering 147
    Word of God 148
    Baptism 151
    Lord's Supper 152
    Funeral 160
    Evening 163
    Special Occasions 166
    Close of Worship 169
Indexes
    Copyright Holders .... [196]
    Anthem Settings of Hymns .... [197]
    Songs Appropriate for Children .... [197]
    Scriptural Index .... [198]
    Topical Index .... [202]
    Authors, Translators, and Souces of Texts ... [214]
    Composers, Arrangers, and Sources of Music .... [217]
    Metrical Index .... [220]
    Tune Names .... [222]
    First Lines and Titles .... [223]

Introduction

New Songs of Rejoicing is a collection of one-hundred seventy-one new hymns, most appearing here for the first time. We have included hymns for all elements and occasions of worship. While not intended as a primary hymnal, it offers the contemporary church many new ways to express faith in God.

Selah Publishing Co. published the hymnal supplement *Songs of Rejoicing: Hymns for Worship, Meditation, and Praise* in 1989, and since its publication, we have continued to find good new texts and tunes. But, more particularly, we have found authors and composers whose work we admire and think deserves wide use. Selah has published a number of individual hymnaries giving the collected works of contemporary poets and composers, and it is hymns from these collections that make up the largest portion of *New Songs of Rejoicing*. This supplement shows our faith in congregational song and how it can move and change the church and her people.

The hymns are organized into sections, beginning with songs for the church seasons, followed by scriptural hymns, hymns on the theme of the Christian in the world, and finally hymns for use in the liturgy of the church. A number of the hymns are given with guitar chords, but keyboard and guitar should not sound together. Topical and scriptural indexes are included to aid in hymn selection.

These poets and composers have much to say to the church today at the end of the century. We are publishing this hymnal because we firmly believe that these hymns have a great deal to offer the church and those who sing them. It is when we sing these hymns that they will come alive within us, and help us to praise God and understand better, if still only dimly, the mystery of God's love and grace.

David P. Schaap, editor

Abbreviations & Symbols

alt.	altered
adapt.	adapted by
arr.	arranged by
b.	born
c.	circa (around)
cent.	century
CM	common meter (86 86)
CMD	common meter double
harm.	harmonized by
LM	long meter (88 88)
PM	peculiar meter
para.	paraphrased by
rev.	revised
SM	short meter (66 86)
st.	stanza(s)
tr.	translated by
vers.	versified by

ADVENT

O Child of Promise, Come!   1

1. O Child of promise, come! O come, Emmanuel! Come, prince of peace, to David's throne; come, God, with us to dwell!
2. The Lord's true Servant, come, in whom is his delight, on whom his holy Spirit rests, the Gentiles' promised light!
3. O come, anointed One, to show blind eyes your face! Good tidings to the poor announce; proclaim God's year of grace!
4. O Man of sorrows, come, despised and cast aside! O bear our griefs, and by your wounds redeem us from our pride!

5. O come, God's holy Lamb,
to death be meekly led!
O save the many by your blood,
for sin so gladly shed!

6. O come, Messiah King,
to reign in endless light,
when heav'nly peace at last goes forth
from Zion's holy height!

Text: James Quinn, S.J., ©. Selah Publishing Co., Inc., U.S. agent.
Music: *The Good Old Songs*, alt.; harm Jack Noble White (from *Songs for the People of God*).
© 1994, Selah Publishing Co., Inc. All rights reserved.

SM
LITTLE MARLBOROUGH

ADVENT
2 Isaiah the Prophet

Text: Joy F. Patterson, 1982. © 1982, The Hymn Society, TCU, Fort Worth, TX 76129. All rights reserved. Used by permission.
Music: *The Southern Harmony*, 1835; harm. Austin C. Lovelace, 1979.
Harm. © 1994, Selah Publishing Co., Inc. All rights reserved.

Irregular
SAMANTHRA

ADVENT

3 Told of God's Favor

1 Told of God's favor, told of God's purpose, Mary said,
"Tell me, how can this be?" Told of the Spirit,
told of the power, told of the promise, Mary said yes.

2 Yes to conceiving, yes to the body changing and
growing, yes to the flesh— yes to the new life
kicking within her, yes to the pleasure, yes to the pain.

3 Yes to the waiting, yes to the labor, yes to the
hurting, yes to the birth— yes to the baby,
yes to the future, yes to the holy, yes to the world.

4 Told of Christ Jesus, told of the Spirit, can we say
yes as Mary said yes? Yes for our bodies,
yes for our spirits, yes for the future, yes for right now.

5 Praise to the Spirit, praise to the Most High sending the
word that Mary was told. Praise to Christ Jesus,
who was made welcome into our world when Mary said yes.

Text: Richard Leach, 1992.
Music: Russell Schulz-Widmar, 1994.
  Text and music © 1994, Selah Publishing Co., Inc. All rights reserved.

10 9 10 9
BORDY

My Soul Proclaims with Wonder

ADVENT 4

Text: *Magnificat* (*Song of Mary*) from Luke 1:46-55); para. by Carl P. Daw, Jr., 1989.
© 1989, Hope Publishing Co., Carol Stream, IL 60188. All rights reserved. Used by permission.
Music: William P. Rowan, 1993. © 1993, Selah Publishing Co., Inc. All rights reserved.

76 76 D with refrain
HUNT

ADVENT

5 Blessed Be the God of Israel

1 Blessed be the God of Is-ra-el, the ev-er-liv-ing Lord.
You come in power to save your own, your peo-ple Is-ra-el.

2 Through ho-ly proph-ets did you speak your word in days of old,
that you would save us from our foes and all who bear us ill.

3 Of old you gave your sol-emn oath to fa-ther A-bra-ham:
whose seed a might-y race should be, and blessed for-ev-er-more.

4 O ti-ny Child, your name shall be the proph-et of the Lord;
the way of God you shall pre-pare to make God's com-ing known.

5 The ris-ing sun shall shine on us to bring the light of day
to all who sit in dark-est night and shad-ow of the grave.

Text: *Song of Zechariah* (Luke 1:67-69); para. James Quinn, S.J., 1969, 1985, ©. Selah Publishing Co., Inc., U.S. agent.
Music: *English Country Songs*, 1893; arr. and harm. Ralph Vaughan Williams, 1906.

CMD
FOREST GREEN

ADVENT
6 Young Mary Lived in Nazareth

Text: Rae E. Whitney, 1982. © 1990, Selah Publishing Co., Inc. All rights reserved.
Music: David W. Music, 1994. © 1994 Selah Publishing Co., Inc. All rights reserved.

CMD
BALLAD OF MARY

CHRISTMAS

When God's Time Had Ripened   8

1 When God's time had ripened, Mary's womb bore fruit, scion of the Godhead, sprung from Jesse's root: so the True Vine branches from the lily's stem, the Rose without blemish blooms in Bethlehem.
2 More than mind can fathom, limit, or untwine, this mysterious yoking, human and divine; but what reason fetters faith at length unlocks, and wise hearts discover truth in paradox.
3 As the Bread of heaven, that we might be fed, chose a manger cradle in the House of Bread, so has Life Eternal mingled with our mortal nature to confound the tomb.
4 For this swaddled infant in a humble place holds our hope of glory and our means of grace; in the Love enfleshed here dawns the world's rebirth, promise of salvation, pledge of peace on earth.

Text: Carl P. Daw, Jr., 1989. © 1990, Hope Publishing Co., Carol Stream, IL 60188. All rights reserved. Used by permission.   65 65 D
Music: Alfred V. Fedak, 1990. © 1990, Selah Publishing Co., Inc. All rights reserved.   ROSE OF BETHLEHEM

CHRISTMAS

9 Away with Our Fears

1. A-way with our fears! the God-head ap-pears, in Christ re-con-ciled the Fath-er of Mer-cies in Je-sus the child.
2. He came from a-bove, in man-i-fest Love, the de-sire of our eyes; the meek Lamb of God, in a man-ger he lies.
3. Made flesh for our sake, that we might par-take the na-ture di-vine, and a-gain in his im-age, his ho-li-ness shine.
4. Then let us be-lieve and glad-ly re-ceive the tid-ings they bring who pub-lish to sin-ners their Sav-ior and King.
5. And while we are here, our King shall ap-pear, his spir-it im-part, and form his full im-age of love in our heart.

Text: Charles Wesley, *Nativity Hymns*, 1745.
Music: Carlton R. Young, 1993. © 1994 Selah Publishing Co., Inc. All rights reserved.

55 56 55
ROBERT

CHRISTMAS

The Babe in Beth'lem's Manger Laid 10

1. The babe in Beth-'lem's manger laid in humble form so low; by wondering angels is surveyed, through all his scenes of woe:
2. A Savior! Sinners all around sing, shout, the wondrous word; let every bosom hail the sound, a Savior, Christ the Lord:
3. For not to sit on David's throne with worldly pomp and joy, he came on earth sinners to atone, and Satan to destroy:
4. Well may we sing a Savior's birth, who need the grace so giv'n, and hail his coming down to earth, who raises us to heaven:

No-well, No-well, No-well now sing, a Savior now is born! No-well, No-well, No-well now sing! And hail this blessed morn!

Text and music: Mark Sedio, 1988. © 1994, Selah Publishing Co., Inc. All rights reserved.
Text and music © 1994, Selah Publishing Co., Inc. All rights reserved.

CM with refrain
AUSE

CHRISTMAS
11 A Babe Is Born

1 A babe is born in Bethlehem, a rose of Jesse's stem. The Virgin Mary's little child, God's Son so sweet and mild. Here in a manger lay your head, a stable for your bed. Come down to us and be our guest, O Savior, ever blest.

2 And when the shepherds heard the song the angels sang that night, their hearts were filled with fear and dread, as heaven filled with light. "Fear not," the angels sang, "fear not. Peace be to all the earth. Rise up and hasten to the child and see this holy birth."

3 They ran, rejoicing, to the child and found him lying there beside the donkey and the lambs, beneath the gleaming star. They knelt in wonder at his side and praised the Lord above for sending them Emmanuel, the babe whom we call Love.

Text: St. 1, Ett barn är födt; tr. Gracia Grindal; st. 2-3 Gracia Grindal, 1992.
Music: Wayne L. Wold, 1994.
Text and music © 1994, Selah Publishing Co., Inc. All rights reserved.

CMD
BLARSON

CHRISTMAS

Hope Is a Star   12

1 Hope is a star that shines in the night, leading us on till the morning is bright.
2 Peace is a ribbon that circles the earth, giving a promise of safety and worth.
3 Joy is a song that welcomes the dawn, telling the world that the Savior is born.
4 Love is a flame that burns in our heart, Jesus has come and will never depart.

Refrain
When God is a child there's joy in our song. The last shall be first, and the weak shall be strong, and none shall be afraid.

Text: Brian Wren, 1987. © 1989, Hope Publishing Co., Carol Stream, IL 60188. All rights reserved. Used by permission.
Music: William P. Rowan, 1993. © 1993 Selah Publishing Co., Inc. All rights reserved.

Irregular
SEYMOUR

CHRISTMAS 14

If I Could Visit Bethlehem

1 If I could visit Bethlehem, what presents would I bring?
   If I could see what happened then, what would I say or sing?

2 I wouldn't take a modern toy, but gold to pay for bread,
   some wine to give his parents' joy, and wool to warm his bed.

3 I'd learn some simple words to speak in Aramaic tongue.
   I'd cradle him, and kiss his cheek, and say, "I'm glad you've come."

4 If Mary asked me who I was and what her child would do,
   I wouldn't talk about the cross, or tell her all I knew.

5 I'd say "He'll never hurt or kill,
   and joy will follow tears.
   We'll know his name and love him still
   in twenty-hundred years."

6 I cannot visit Bethlehem,
   but what I can, I'll do:
   I'll love you, Jesus, as my friend,
   and give my life to you.

Text: Brian Wren, 1988. © 1990, Hope Publishing Co., Carol Stream, IL 60188. All rights reserved. Used by permission.
Music: William P. Rowan, 1992. © 1993, Selah Publishing Co., Inc. All rights reserved.

CM
SIMMONS

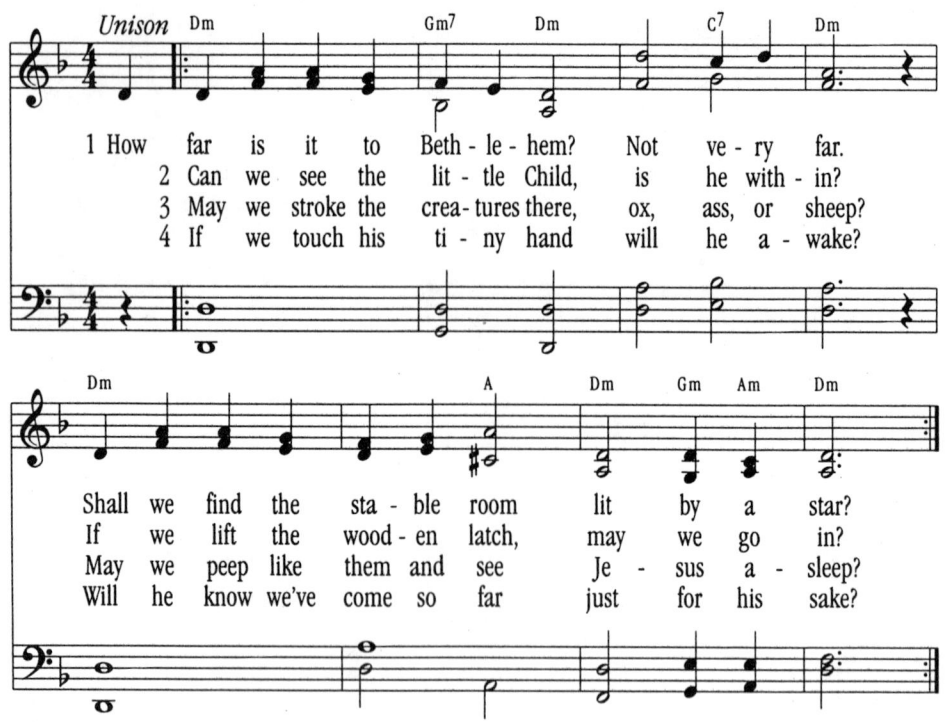

CHRISTMAS

15 How Far Is It to Bethlehem?

1. How far is it to Bethlehem? Not very far.
Shall we find the stable room lit by a star?

2. Can we see the little Child, is he within?
If we lift the wooden latch, may we go in?

3. May we stroke the creatures there, ox, ass, or sheep?
May we peep like them and see Jesus asleep?

4. If we touch his tiny hand will he awake?
Will he know we've come so far just for his sake?

Text: Frances Chesterton.
Music: William S. Haynie, 1993. © 1994, Selah Publishing Co., Inc. All rights reserved.

74 74
STABLE ROOM

EPIPHANY/LIFE OF CHRIST

That King before Whose Majesty 16

1. That King, before whose majesty the fire-bright angels tremble still, is now a babe in Mary's arms, and subject to a mother's will.
2. Earth is his footstool, yet her home is all the universe he sees; the Lord of Lords— a little child— explores his world on hands and knees.
3. How new the helplessness of God! The action, terrifying, bold! And how prophetic were those gifts of myrrh and frankincense and gold!
4. For, when the Wise Men worshipped him and offered presents from the East, such gifts paid homage to a king who is both sacrifice and priest.
5. At Christ's profound humility both earth and heaven in wonder gaze; this Child, the Incarnate Word of God, is worthy of all highest praise!

Text: Rae E. Whitney, 1986.
Music: *The Southern Harmony*, 1835; harm. Jack Noble White, 1982 (from *Songs for the People of God*).
Text and harm. © 1994, Selah Publishing Co., Inc. All rights reserved.

LM
PROSPECT

EPIPHANY/LIFE OF CHRIST

17 Sing of God Made Manifest

1 Sing of God made man-i-fest in a child ro-bust and blest,
to whose home in Beth-le-hem, where a star had guid-ed them,
ma-gi came and gifts un-bound, signs mys-te-rious and pro-found:
myrrh and frank-in-cense and gold, grave and God and king fore-told.

2 Sing of God made man-i-fest when at Jor-dan John con-fessed,
"I should be bap-tized by you, but your bid-ding I will do."
Then from heaven a dou-ble sign— dove-like Spir-it, voice di-vine—
hailed the true A-noint-ed One: "This is my be-lov-ed Son."

3 Sing of God made man-i-fest when Christ came as wed-ding-guest
and at Ca-na gave a sign, turn-ing wa-ter in-to wine;
fur-ther still was love re-vealed as he taught, for-gave, and healed,
bring-ing light and life to all who would lis-ten to God's call.

4 Sing of God made man-i-fest on the cloud-capped moun-tain's crest,
where the Law and Proph-ets waned so that Christ a-lone re-mained:
glimpse of glo-ry, pledge of grace, given as Je-sus set his face
towards the wait-ing cross and grave, sign of hope that God would save.

Text: Carl P. Daw, Jr., 1989. © 1990, Hope Publishing Co., Carol Stream, IL 60188. All rights reserved. Used by permission.
Music: Roy Hopp, 1990. © 1990, Selah Publishing Co., Inc. All rights reserved.

77 77 D
TURNBERRY

EPIPHANY/LIFE OF CHRIST

O Joseph   18

6 O Joseph, did you teach him wood—
  taught you his first vocation?
  Yes, and at length he took up wood
  and crafted our salvation!

7 O Lord, could we be saints like him—
  trusting, obedient, caring?
  Yes, help our lives and lips proclaim
  the tidings you came bearing!

Text: Maureen O'Brien and David A. Robb, 1985. © 1994, Selah Publishing Co., Inc. All rights reserved.
Music: William P. Rowan, 1985. © 1993, Selah Publishing Co., Inc. All rights reserved.

87 87
CARPENTER

EPIPHANY/LIFE OF CHRIST

19   O Lord, Eternal Light of God

1. O Lord, eternal Light of God, who shone before the stars or sun, bid darkness flee: "Let there be light within the hearts of everyone!"
2. O patient Light of Galilee, whose presence brought the blind their sight, dispel the dread of darkened days; grant us the will to live in light!
3. O loving Light of Calvary, who shone when sun at noon refused, beam forth forgiveness from your cross till we can love, although abused.
4. O promised Light forevermore proceeding from the timeless throne, shine more and more till perfect day reveals your light where yet unknown.

Text: David A. Robb, 1982.
Music: Trad. English carol; *Christmas Carols Ancient and Modern*, 1833; harm. Jeffrey Rickard, 1992.
Text and harm. © 1994, Selah Publishing Co., Inc. All rights reserved.

LM
CORNISH CAROL

EPIPHANY/LIFE OF CHRIST

Who Better Than Mary 20

5 When Jesus had risen and gone to the Father,
  she shared with his friends in the breaking of bread. *Refrain*

6 Whenever the Church is unloving, divided,
  the wounds bleed afresh in the body of Christ. *Refrain*

7 Whoever brings love to the sick and the dying,
  like Mary, gives comfort to bodies and souls. *Refrain*

8 Lord, we never saw you in prison or homeless,
  Yet, when we helped others we know we helped you. *Refrain*

Text: Rae E. Whitney, 1978.
Music: Alec Wyton, 1994.
Text and music © 1994, Selah Publishing Co., Inc. All rights reserved.

12 11 11 9
RIDGEFIELD

EPIPHANY/LIFE OF CHRIST

21 Woman in the Night

1. Woman in the night, spent from giving birth,
guard our precious light: peace is on the earth!
Woman in the crowd, creeping up behind,
find your friends and tell: drink your heart's desire!

2. Woman at the well, question the Messiah:
find your friends and tell: drink your heart's desire!
Woman at the feast, let the righteous stare:
Christ needs loving still, though your hope is dead.

3. Women on the hill, stand when men have fled!
Christ needs loving still, though your hope is dead.
Women in the dawn, care and spices bring:
leave your second place: listen, think, and speak!

4. Woman in the house, nurtured to be meek,
leave your second place: listen, think, and speak!
Woman on the road, welcomed and restored,

Text: Brian Wren, 1982. © 1983, Hope Publishing Co., Carol Stream, IL 60188. All rights reserved. Used by permission.
Music: Alfred V. Fedak, 1989. © 1990, Selah Publishing Co., Inc. All rights reserved.

55 55 D with refrain
NEW DISCIPLES

EPIPHANY/LIFE OF CHRIST

22 Woman in the Night

1. Woman in the night, spent from giving birth, guard our precious light: peace is on the earth!
2. Woman in the crowd, creeping up behind, touching is allowed: seek and you will find!
3. Woman at the well, question the Messiah; find your friends and tell; drink your heart's desire!
4. Woman at the feast, let the righteous stare; come and go in peace; love him with your hair!

Refrain
Come and join the song, women, children, men.

Text: Brian Wren, 1982. © 1983, Hope Publishing Co., Carol Stream, IL 60188. All rights reserved. Used by permission
Music: William P. Rowan, 1985. © 1992, Selah Publishing Co., Inc. All rights reserved.

55 55 with refrain
WICKLUND

Je - sus makes us free to live a - gain!

5. Woman in the house,
   nurtured to be meek,
   leave your second place:
   listen, think, and speak!
   Refrain

6. Women on the road,
   welcomed and restored,
   travel far and wide;
   witness to the Lord!
   Refrain

7. Women on the hill,
   stand when men have fled!
   Christ needs loving still,
   though your hope is dead.
   Refrain

8. Women in the dawn,
   care and spices bring;
   earliest to mourn;
   earliest to sing!
   Refrain

EPIPHANY/LIFE OF CHRIST

23 We Have Come at Christ's Own Bidding

1 We have come at Christ's own bid-ding to this high and ho-ly place,
2 Light breaks in up-on our dark-ness; splen-dor bathes the flesh-joined Word;
3 Strength-ened by this glimpse of glo-ry, fear-ful lest our faith de-cline,

where we wait with hope and long-ing for some tok-en of God's grace.
Mos-es and E-li-jah mar-vel as the heaven-ly voice is heard.
we like Pe-ter find it tempt-ing to re-main and build a shrine.

Here we pray for new as-sur-ance that our faith is not in vain,
Eyes and hearts be-hold with won-der how the Law and Proph-ets meet:
But true wor-ship gives us cour-age to pro-claim what we pro-fess,

Text: Carl P. Daw, Jr., 1990. © 1988, Hope Publishing Co., Carol Stream, IL 60188. All rights reserved. Used by permission.
Music: David Ashley White, 1991. © 1991, Selah Publishing Co., Inc. All rights reserved.

87 87 D
BREWER

searching like those first disciples for a sign both clear and plain.
Christ, with garments drenched in brightness, stands transfigured and complete.
that our daily lives may prove us people of the God we bless.

EPIPHANY/LIFE OF CHRIST
O Carpenter 24

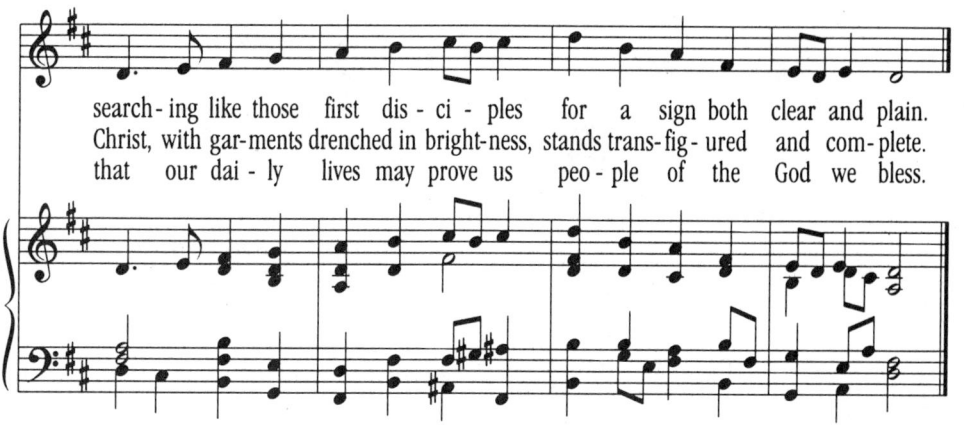

1. O carpenter, why leave the bench where wood yields to your art,
2. O carpenter, why leave the tools to carry out your plans,
3. O carpenter, why leave the world of table, bed, and house,
4. O carpenter, why leave repairs with wood and clamp and glue,
5. O carpenter, who else could do the work that you have done?

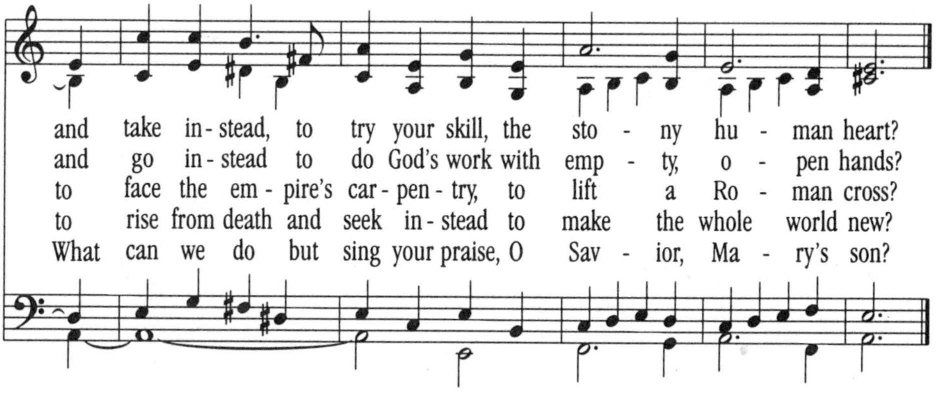

and take instead, to try your skill, the stony human heart?
and go instead to do God's work with empty, open hands?
to face the empire's carpentry, to lift a Roman cross?
to rise from death and seek instead to make the whole world new?
What can we do but sing your praise, O Savior, Mary's son?

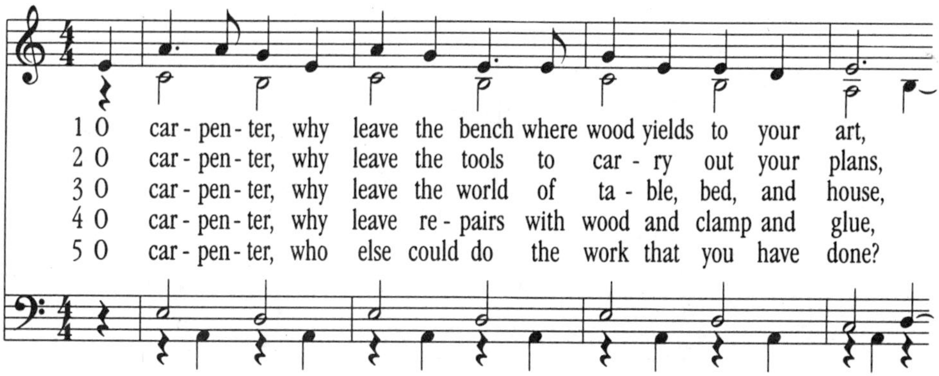

Text: Richard Leach, 1988.
Music: Wilbur Held, 1993.
Text and music © 1994, Selah Publishing Co., Inc. All rights reserved.

CM
O CARPENTER

LENT
27 Where Was the Greater Struggle?

1 Where was the greater struggle? Where Jesus, Spirit-blessed, / was driven by the Spirit into the wilderness?
2 Where was the greater struggle? Where Satan's ways were bare, / in wild and empty places when Jesus met them there?
3 Where was the greater struggle? Where Jesus' company / was animal or angel before his ministry?
4 In wilderness Christ Jesus rehearsed for what would come, / and won a lesser struggle before a greater one.

Text: Richard Leach, 1992 (based on Mark 1:12-13).
Music: Hal H. Hopson, 1990.
Text and music © 1994, Selah Publishing Co., Inc. All rights reserved.

76 76 D
CORNING

Or was it in his home town, con-front-ed by the wise,
Or in the crowd-ed ci-ty, where Sa-tan's words and ways
Or was the strug-gle great-er where Je-sus walked with friends,
O Je-sus, we would join you in wil-der-ness and town,

who said that Je-sus' spir-it came from the Lord of Flies?
were hid-den like a leav-en with-in its life each day?
and sought to teach and lead them and love them till the end?
that we may share your strug-gle in Lent and all year 'round.

This hymn may be sung in two-part canon *a capella* at a distance of one measure.

28 Sovereign Maker of All Things

Unison

1. Sovereign Maker of all things, God of covenant and grace,
every creature knows your power, quakes with fear before your face.
But your mercy far exceeds what our minds can comprehend;
deep compassion stays your hand, chastening not, though we offend.

2. You have promised to forgive contrite sinners who repent;
so I come with humbled heart, by your word made confident.
I have sinned, Lord, I have sinned: well I know my wickedness.
Yet I make this prayer to you: Lord, forgive me, heal, and bless.

3. Let me not be lost in sin, banished to eternal night;
God who hears the penitent, let your goodness show your might.
Though I be unworthy, Lord, your great mercy will I claim,
till I join the hosts above who forever praise your name.

Text: *Prayer of Manasseh*; para. Carl P. Daw, Jr., 1990. © 1990, Hope Publishing Co., Carol Stream, IL 60188. All rights reserved. Used by permission.
Music: Alfred V. Fedak, 1988. © 1989, Selah Publishing Co., Inc. All rights reserved.

77 77 D
DANCE OF GRACE

Hosanna, Hosanna!

LENT 29

1. Ho-san-na, ho-san-na! the cheer-ing peo-ple cry,
   ho-san-na, ho-san-na! as Je-sus pas-ses by.
   Mes-si-ah, Is-rael's sav-ior! All hail to Dav-id's son!
   In God's name he is com-ing, the blest and chos-en One!

2. Their palm branch-es wav-ing, the crowds press near to see
   what man-ner of king God's own Chos-en One will be—
   he rides a bor-rowed don-key, his cloth-ing poor and plain;
   no rich-es, no great splen-dor, will greet his com-ing reign.

3. The crowds that have cheered him too soon will fall a-way;
   his friends all will leave him, too filled with fear to stay.
   The sol-diers come to seize him, by rul-ers he'll be tried;
   his in-no-cence con-demns him; he must be cru-ci-fied.

4. We, too, cry ho-san-na! and cel-e-brate this day,
   for death can-not hold him; he lives, with us to stay.
   God, strength-en us and guide us who call him Lord and Friend,
   that we may walk be-side him un-til this life shall end.

Text and music: Joy F. Patterson, 1994.
Text and music © 1994, Selah Publishing Co., Inc. All rights reserved.

12 12 13 13
DUANE

LENT

30 Now Let Us All with One Accord

1. Now let us all with one accord, in company with ages past, keep vigil with our
heavenly Lord in his temptation and his fast.

2. The covenant, so long revealed to those of
faith in former time, Christ by his own ex-
ample sealed, the Lord of love, in love sublime.

3. Your love, O Lord, our sinful race has not returned, but falsified; Author of mercy,
turn your face and grant repentance for our pride.

4. Remember, Lord, though frail we be, in your own
image were we made; help us, lest in anxi-e-ty,
we cause your Name to be betrayed.

5. Therefore, we pray you, Lord, forgive; so when our
wanderings here shall cease, we may with you forever live, in love and unity and peace.

Text: Attr. Gregory the Great, 6th cent.; tr. James Quinn, S.J., 1972, ©. Selah Publishing Co., Inc., U.S. agent.
Music: *Hesperian Harp*, 1848, attr. Freeman Lewis; harm. Louise McAllister, 1958.

LM
BOURBON

With the Body That Was Broken

LENT 31

1. With the Body that was broken, to the Body who proclaim,
by the Blood that is life's token, for the life found in his Name:
so the Word-made-flesh has spoken, and his presence here we claim.

2. In the cross of Christ confiding, by the cross we bear as sign,
through the Spirit's gifts and guiding, with these gifts of bread and wine:
so the Church in faith abiding keeps the feast Christ made divine.

3. Fed by breaking and outpouring, joined in breaking-forth of praise,
given the peace of God's restoring, sent in peace to live always:
so we show forth our adoring as God's servants all our days.

Text: Carl P. Daw, Jr., 1985. © 1989, Hope Publishing Co., Carol Stream, IL 60188. All rights reserved. Used by permission.
Music: David Ashley White, 1985. © 1994, Selah Publishing Co., Inc. All rights reserved.

87 87 87
ST. MARK'S CHAPEL

LENT
32   Three Tall Trees Grew on a Windy Hill

1 Three tall trees grew on a wind-y hill close by a He-brew town; where once a wood had proud-ly stood now the rest of the trees were down.

2 One day there came to that wind-y hill, those who were seek-ing wood. Their hands reached out to work their will where the last of the trees still stood.

3 sea-sons passed on that win-dy hill close by a He-brew town. That man-ger cra-dled a ba-by still, and a star in the east looked down.

4 voice cried, "Halt," and a pris-oner stood, bleed-ing and bound and still, while they chose for his cross the last of the wood that had grown on that wind-y hill.

5 dark-ness came on the cru-el hill sil-enc-ing grief and pain, and it seemed that the heart of the world was still, and it nev-er would wake a-gain.

"A cra-dle," said one, "for a did they fash-ion a
And when as a teach-er he
It had cra-dled a ba-by a-
But a war was fought in the

Text: Herbert O'Driscoll, ©. Used by permission.
Music: Alfred V. Fedak, 1989. © 1989 Selah Publishing Co., Inc. All rights reserved.

Irregular
THREE TALL TREES

1. child I will be." "As a ship," said another, "I will sail the sea. "I will stay," said the third, "I will stand strong and free, still pointing to God on high."

2. manger stall, from another the keel of a fish-boat small, but the third they laid by a workshop wall, so straight did it stand, and high.

3. The spoke on the shore, that boat was brought and the Lord it bore, and across the waters he taught them more of love, and a God on high.

4. A sleep and awake, it had held the sail on the stormy lake: now it bore him aloft for the whole world's sake, the Son of God most high.

5. Deep silent hours from the gates of hell up to heaven's towers, till death was robbed of its awful powers and Jesus rose on high.

LENT
33 How Shallow Former Shadows Seem

1 How shallow former shadows seem beside this great reverse, as darkness swallows up the Light of all the universe: creation shivers at the shock; the Temple rends its veil; a pallid stillness stifles time; and nature's motions fail.

2 This is no midday fantasy, no flight of fevered brain. With vengeance awful, grim, and real, chaos is come again: the hands that formed us from the soil are nailed upon the cross; the Word that gave us life and breath expires in utter loss.

3 Yet deep within this darkness lives a Love so fierce and free that arcs all voids and— risk supreme!—embraces agony. Its perfect testament is etched in iron, blood, and wood; with awe we glimpse its true import and dare to call it

Text: Carl P. Daw, Jr., 1990. © 1990, Hope Publishing Co., Inc., Carol Stream, IL 60188. All rights reserved. Used by permission.
Music: William P. Rowan, 1990. © 1993, Selah Publishing Co., Inc. All rights reserved.

CMD
CARDINAL

What Are These Wounds

LENT 34

Text: Rae E. Whitney, 1981, based on Zechariah 13:6.
Music: Amanda Husberg, 1994.
Text and music © 1994, Selah Publishing Co., Inc. All rights reserved.

1. What are these wounds in your hands, dear Savior? What are these wounds in your hands? "These are the wounds with which I was wounded, here in the house of my friends."
2. What are these wounds in your feet, dear Savior? What are these wounds in your feet? "These are the wounds with which I was wounded, here in the house of my friends."
3. What are these wounds on your brow, dear Savior? What are these wounds on your brow? "These are the wounds with which I was wounded, here in the house of my friends."
4. What are these wounds in your side, dear Savior? What are these wounds in your side? "These are the wounds with which I was wounded, here in the house of my friends."
5. What are these wounds in your heart, dear Savior? What are these wounds in your heart? "These are the wounds with which I was wounded, here in the house of my friends."

10 7 10 7
MIKHAEL GIDEON JACOB

EASTER

35 The Tomb Is Empty!

1 The tomb is emp-ty! Come and see where once the bod-y lay.
2 The tomb is emp-ty! Come and hear these words of life and peace:
3 The tomb is emp-ty! Come and touch the stone and fold-ed shroud.
4 The tomb is emp-ty! Come and meet the Ris-en Christ, our Lord

Can it be true that Je-sus Christ is raised to life to-day?
"He is not here. He lives a-gain in all your Gal-i-lees."
Christ lives in-deed. Al-le-lu-ia! Be-liev-ers, shout a-loud.
in whom we have our vic-to-ry, in whom is life re-stored.

Optional organ accompaniment for stanza 4

Text: Sylvia Dunstan, 1988. © 1991, G.I.A. Publications. Used by permission.
Music: David Ashley White, 1992. © 1994, Selah Publishing Co., Inc. All rights reserved.

CM
WINSTON

Make Songs of Joy

EASTER 36

1. Make songs of joy to Christ, our head; Alleluia! he lives again who once was dead! Alleluia!
2. Our life was purchased by his loss; Alleluia! he died our death upon the cross. Alleluia!
3. O death, where is your deadly sting? Alleluia! Assumed by our triumphant King! Alleluia!
4. And where your victory, O grave, Alleluia! when one like Christ has come to save? Alleluia!

Text: Jiri Tranousky, 17th cent; tr. Jaroslav J. Vajda. Tr. © 1978, *Lutheran Book of Worship*.
Reprinted by permission of Augsburg Fortress.
Music: AnnaMae Meyer Bush, 1993. © 1994, Selah Publishing Co., Inc. All rights reserved.

84 84
VICTORY

EASTER

37 When Lazarus Lay within the Tomb

1. When Lazarus lay within the tomb, held fast in bonds of death, the voice of Jesus brought him forth, restored to life and breath.
2. When time and change bring down our world like shards of shattered glass, all hope seems crushed in bleak despair, a night that will not pass.
3. Yet through our anger, fear, and grief our Lord stands always near, shares all our anguish, helps us lift the load of pain we bear.
4. Still Jesus calls, "Come forth and live!" For freedom we were born: throw off the graveclothes of despair this resurrection morn!

(G♯ on final stanza)

Text: Joy F. Patterson, 1993.
Music: David Ashley White, 1969, rev. 1993.
Text and music © 1994, Selah Publishing Co., Inc. All rights reserved.

CM
SUMTER

ASCENSION AND REIGN

Praise Him As He Mounts the Skies   38

1 Praise him as he mounts the skies, Al-le-lu-ia! Christ, the Lord of Paradise! Al-le-lu-ia! Cry hosanna in the height, Al-le-lu-ia! as he rises out of sight! Al-le-lu-ia!

2 Now at last he takes his throne, Al-le-lu-ia! from all ages his alone! Al-le-lu-ia! With his praise creation rings: Al-le-lu-ia! "Lord of lords and King of Kings!" Al-le-lu-ia!

3 Hands and feet and side reveal Al-le-lu-ia! wounds of love, high priest-hood's seal! Al-le-lu-ia! Advocate for us he pleads; Al-le-lu-ia! heavenly Priest, he intercedes! Al-le-lu-ia!

4 Christians, raise your eyes above! Al-le-lu-ia! He will come again in love, Al-le-lu-ia! on that great and wondrous day Al-le-lu-ia! when this world will pass away! Al-le-lu-ia!

5 At his word new heavens and earth Al-le-lu-ia! will in glory spring to birth! Al-le-lu-ia! Risen Lord, our great amen, Al-le-lu-ia! come, Lord Jesus, come again! Alleluia!

Text: James Quinn, S.J., ©. Selah Publishing Co., Inc., U.S. agent.
Music: Ray W. Urwin, 1994. © 1994, Selah Publishing Co., Inc. All rights reserved.

74 74 74 74
FENTON

ASCENSION AND REIGN

39 Christ the King, Enthroned in Splendor

Unison

1. Christ the King, enthroned in splendor, comes from heaven to be our priest! One with him as priest and victim, one in love, we share his feast! Praise him in high heaven above! Praise him in this feast of love!

2. Light here scatters all our darkness! Life here triumphs over death! Come, receive from Christ in glory God the Spirit's living breath! Praise Christ for his victory won! Praise the Father's firstborn Son!

3. Heaven is here! The gracious Father gives to us his only Son! Here is sent the loving Spirit, making all in Christ but one! Praise the Father, praise the Son, praise the Spirit, Godhead one!

Text: James Quinn, S.J., 1969, ©. Selah Publishing Co., Inc., U. S. agent.
Music: Keith Landis, 1988; harm. Jeffrey Rickard, 1988. © 1992, Hope Publishing Co., Carol Stream, IL 60188.
All rights reserved. Used by permission.

87 87 77
LATIMER

PENTECOST AND THE HOLY SPIRIT

Come Holy Spirit, Revive Your Church   40

1. Come, Holy Spirit, revive your church with flames of living fire.
2. Come, Holy Spirit, and give us words as mighty as the wind
3. Come, Holy Spirit, refresh us now by water and the Word.
4. Come, Holy Spirit, send wind and fire and set your church aflame

   Ignite our witness, and with your love, our weary hearts inspire.
   to raise up preachers to preach good news to those weighed down by sin.
   Cut back the vineyard, which cannot live without your two-edged sword.
   to preach the Gospel so all the world may hear your holy name.

   Come, Holy Spirit, revive your church with flames of living fire.
   Come, Holy Spirit, and give us words as mighty as the wind.
   Come, Holy Spirit, refresh us now by water and the Word.
   Come, Holy Spirit, send wind and fire and set your church aflame.

Text: Gracia Grindal, 1988.
Music: David Ashley White, 1994.
Text and music © 1994, Selah Publishing Co., Inc. All rights reserved.

86 96 86
AUSTIN

PENTECOST AND THE HOLY SPIRIT

41   Holy Spirit, Truth Divine

1. Holy Spirit, truth divine, dawn upon this soul of mine;
Word of God and inward light, wake my spirit, clear my sight.

2. Holy Spirit, love divine, glow within this heart of mine;
kindle every high desire; purge me with your holy fire.

3. Holy Spirit, power divine, fortify this will of mine;
by your will I strongly live, bravely bear, and nobly strive.

4. Holy Spirit, peace divine, still this restless heart of mine;
speak to calm this tossing sea, stayed in your tranquility.

5. Holy Spirit, right divine, King within my conscience reign;
be my guide, and I shall be firmly bound, forever free.

Text: Samuel Longfellow, 1864.
Music: Joel Martinson, 1992. © 1994 Selah Publishing Co., Inc. All rights reserved.

77 77
KESSLER PARK

PENTECOST AND THE HOLY SPIRIT
Dove to Flesh 42

1 Dove to flesh still drip-ping wa-ter on the Jor-dan riv-er bank,
2 Fire to flesh, the men and wo-men on the day of Pent-e-cost,
3 Here are bod-ies, gift-ed, need-y; here is flesh and blood and bone.

dove to flesh like that of sin-ners on the Jor-dan riv-er bank—
fire to flesh like this of ours on the day of Pent-e-cost—
Here are scars and strength and beau-ty; here is flesh and blood and bone.

dove to flesh, the Ho-ly Spir-it came to Je-sus like a dove.
fire to flesh, the Ho-ly Spir-it com-ing down like tongues of fire.
Dove and fire, O Ho-ly Spir-it, come to us that we may sing,

Sing the com-ing of the Spir-it, dove to flesh to fire to flesh.
Sing the com-ing of the Spir-it, dove to flesh to fire to flesh.
sing your com-ing, Ho-ly Spir-it, dove to flesh to fire to flesh.

Text: Richard Leach, 1990. © 1994, Selah Publishing Co., Inc. All rights reserved.
Music: J. Leavitt's *Christian Lyre*, 1830; harm. Ralph Vaughan Williams, 1906.

87 87 D
PLEADING SAVIOR

PSALMS
43 Your Law, O Lord, Is Perfect

1 Your law, O Lord, is perfect, the simple making wise;
how pure are your commandments, enlightening my eyes!

2 More to be sought than riches, your words are my soul's wealth;
their taste is like sweet honey, imparting life and health.

3 My Strength and my Redeemer, Lawgiver and true Light,
my words and meditations make worthy in your sight.

Text: Psalm 19:1-14; para. Keith Landis, 1987.
Music: Trad. English carol; harm. by Peter Cutts, 1987 (from *Songs for the People of God*).
Text and harm. © 1994, Selah Publishing Co., Inc. All rights reserved.

76 76
CHERRY TREE

Since You Are Shepherd

PSALMS 44

Unison

1. Since you are Shep-herd of my life, no good thing is denied: in want or plenty, peace or strife, my needs are all supplied.
2. Since you are Shep-herd of the sheep, your pasture table's spread; green fields and gentle streams shall keep each hungry creature fed.
3. Since you are Shep-herd of the flocks, no evil need I fear; your presence undergirds the shocks; in death's ravine you're near!
4. Since you are Shep-herd of the fold, no hurt from foes endures; your rod and staff will firmly hold till comfort works its cures. you, with you.

5. Since you are Shepherd of the soul,
   with ointment for our woes,
   your paths lead rightly toward that goal
   where mercy overflows.

6. Since you are Shepherd of the heart,
   restoring life anew,
   pursuing love will not depart,
   and I shall dwell with you.

Text: Psalm 23; para. David A. Robb, 1984.
Music: Darcy Hill, 1993; arr. Rusty Edwards, 1993.
Text and music © 1994, Selah Publishing Co., Inc. All rights reserved.

CM
SADIE

PSALMS
45 The Lord My Pasture Shall Prepare

1. The Lord my pasture shall prepare, and feed me with a shepherd's care; his presence shall my wants supply, and guard me with a watchful eye. My noonday walks he shall attend, and all my midnight hours defend.

2. And when I faint on mountain trail, or on hot sands my spirits fail, to fertile vales and dewy meads, my weary, wandering steps he leads, where peaceful rivers, soft and slow, amid the verdant landscape flow.

3. Although in darkest paths I tread, of unknown perils feel no dread. My steadfast heart shall fear no ill; for thou, O Lord, art with me still; thy friendly crook shall give me aid, and gently guide me through the shade.

Text: Psalm 23; para. Joseph Addison, 1713.
Music: Arabic folk song, arr. William S. Haynie, 1993. © 1994, Selah Publishing Co., Inc. All rights reserved.

88 88 88
ARABIA

Who Is This King of Glory?

Antiphon

Who is this king of glo-ry? It is the Lord!

Verses

1. O gates, lift up your heads; grow high-er, an-cient doors. Let him en-ter, the king of glo-ry.
2. Who is the king of glo-ry? The Lord, the might-y, the val-iant, the Lord, the val-iant in bat-tle.
3. O gates, lift high your heads; grow high-er, an-cient doors. Let him en-ter, the king of glo-ry.
4. Who is he, the king of glo-ry? He, the Lord of arm-ies, he is the king of glo-ry.

Text: Psalm 24.
Music: Leo Nestor, 1986. © 1994, Selah Publishing Co., Inc. All rights reserved.

PSALMS
47 How Blessed Are Those

1. How blessed are those whose transgressions are cleansed by the mercies of God, whose sins have been graciously covered by Jesus own suffering and blood. When lost in despair I grow silent and fail to confess all my sin. My bones sigh with in me for mercy; my strength fails like pools in the sun.

2. But when I confess my transgressions and flee to the strength of God's arm, I'm hidden and kept from my terror in spite of the depth of the storm. Be glad, O my soul, for God's mercy; rejoice, and sing songs of great joy, for mercy is compassed around you; be glad in your God, and rejoice!

Text: Psalm 32; vers. Gracia Grindal, 1984.
Music: *The Sacred Harp*. 1844; harm. David N. Johnson, 1977 (from *Songs for the People of God*).
Text and harm. © 1994, Selah Publishing Co., Inc. All rights reserved.

98 98 D
SAWYER'S EXIT

As Panting Deer

PSALMS 48

1 As pant-ing deer de-sire the wa-ter brooks when wan-dering in a dry and des-ert place, so yearns my thirs-ty soul for you, O God, and longs at last to see you face to face.

2 Both day and night my tears have been my food, while scof-fers taunt me, "Where is your God now?" My soul dis-solves as I re-call the throng, whose pil-grim hymns I led to Zi-on's brow.

3 Why are you heav-y-heart-ed, O my soul? And why are you so mired in deep dis-cord? Still put your hope and trust in God a-lone, whom I will praise, my Sav-ior and my Lord.

Text: Psalm 42:1-7; para. Carl P. Daw, Jr., 1985. © 1990, Hope Publishing Co., Carol Stream, IL 60188. All rights reserved. Used by permission.
Music: David Ashley White, 1982. © 1991, Selah Publishing Co., Inc. All rights reserved.

10 10 10 10
WARD

PSALMS
49 In God I Trust

Antiphon

In God I trust; I shall not fear.

Verses

1 Have mercy on me, God; men crush me; they
2 You have kept an ac - count of my wanderings; you have
3 This I know, that God is on my side. In
4 I am bound by the vows I have made you. O

Text: Psalm 55.
Music: Leo Nestor, 1988. © 1994, Selah Publishing Co., Inc. All rights reserved.

fight me all day long and op - press me; my foes crush me
kept a record of my tears. Are they not
God, whose word I praise, in the Lord, whose
God, I will offer you praise; for you rescued me to

all the day long; for many fight proudly a - gainst me.
written in your book? When I call you, my foes are put to flight.
word I praise. What can mortal man do a - gainst me?
walk in your presence, to en - joy the light of the living.

PSALMS
50 Our God Forgives Us

1 Our God forgives us fully of our sin, with-
2 When steadfast love and faithfulness abound, then
3 When righteousness pours down from cloudy skies, then
4 Then peace will make a path before God's feet, a-

draws the wrath which we deserve. God receives us
righteousness and peace will kiss. Faith will blossom
flowers of peace begin to grow. Fruits of faith will
midst the worry and distress. Stubble is re-

once again, with peace and grace our faith restores.
from the ground, and justice bloom with trust and peace.
show increase, and we will reap the love God sows.
stored to wheat, when we the name of God confess.

Text: Psalm 85; vers. Mark Decker, 1986.
Music: Mark Sedio, 1986.
Text and music © 1994, Selah Publishing Co., Inc. All rights reserved.

10 8 7 8
LOWEN

Come, Let Us Raise a Joyful Sound

PSALMS 51

1 Come, let us raise a joyful sound and praise our mighty Lord.
With thankful voices, shout aloud, extol our most high God.

2 Come, worship the creating One, whose hand formed earth and sea,
who counted mountain heights his own, carved cavern majesties.

3 With shepherd love he prods and guides his wandering people home.
In joyous songs let us unite and come before his throne.

4 O let us kneel before our Lord, Creator, Savior, Rock,
and, kneeling, listen to his Word, the wondrous Word of God.

Text: Psalm 95; vers. Mark Sedio, 1984.
Music: Mark Sedio, 1984.
Text and music © 1994, Selah Publishing Co., Inc. All rights reserved.

CM
JOYFUL SONG

PSALMS
52   To God with Gladness Sing

1 To God with glad-ness sing; your rock and Sav-ior bless; with-
2 God cra-dles in his hand the heights and depths of earth; God
3 Your heaven-ly Fath-er praise; ac-claim God's on-ly Son. Your

in God's tem-ple bring your songs of thank-ful-ness! O God of
made the sea and land and brought the world to birth! O God most
voice in hom-age raise to God who makes all one! O Dove of

might, to you we sing, en-throned as King on heav-en's height!
high, we are your sheep; on us you keep your shep-herd's eye!
peace, on us de-scend, that strife may end and joy in-crease!

Text: Psalm 95; para. James Quinn, S.J., ©. Selah Publishing Co., Inc., U.S. agent. All rights reserved.
Music: John Darwall, 1770.

66 66 88
DARWALL'S 148TH

The Lord Has Made Known His Salvation

PSALMS 53

Sing to the Lord a <u>new</u> song,
for he has done marve<u>lous</u> things.
With his right hand and his <u>holy</u> arm
has he won for him<u>self</u> the victory. *Refrain*

The Lord has made known <u>his</u> victory;
his righteousness has he openly shown in the sight of <u>the</u> nations.
He remembers his mercy and faithfulness to the <u>house</u> of Israel,
and all the ends of the earth have seen the victory <u>of</u> our God. *Refrain*

Shout with joy to the Lord, all <u>you</u> lands;
lift up your voice, rejoice <u>and</u> sing.
Sing to the Lord <u>with</u> the harp,
with the harp and the <u>voice</u> of song. *Refrain*

With trumpets and the sound of <u>the</u> horn
shout with joy before the King, <u>the</u> Lord.
Let the sea make a noise and all <u>that</u> is in it,
the lands and those who <u>dwell</u> therein. *Refrain*

Let the rivers clap <u>their</u> hands, (1)
and let the hills ring out with joy before <u>the</u> Lord, (1)
when he comes to judge <u>the</u> earth. (2)
In righteousness shall he <u>judge</u> the world (3)
and the peo<u>ples</u> with equity. (4) *Refrain*

The intonation is played. Cantor sings refrain. All repeat refrain. Cantor sings verses. All sing refrain after each group of verses. In the psalm-tone the singer leaves the reciting note on the underlined word or syllable.

Text: Psalm 98.
Music: George Black, 1983. © Anglican Book Centre. Used by permission.

PSALMS
54 Send Forth Your Spirit, O Lord

Refrain: Send forth your Spir-it, O Lord, and re-new the face of the earth.

O Lord, how manifold are <u>your</u> works! (1)
in wisdom you have made <u>them</u> all; (2)
the earth is full of <u>your</u> creatures. (3)
Yonder is the great and <u>wide</u> sea (1)
with its living creatures too many <u>to</u> number, (2)
creatures both <u>small</u> and great. (4) *Refrain*

Text: Psalm 104:25-35.
Music: George Black, 1987. © Anglican Book Centre. Used by permission.

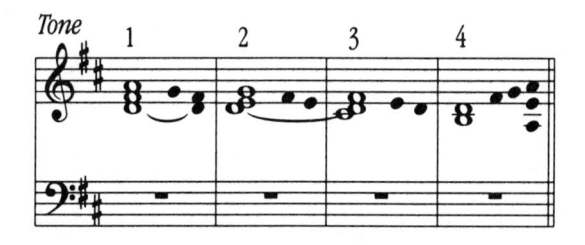

There move <u>the</u> ships, (1)
and there is that <u>Le</u>viathan, (2)
which you have made for <u>the</u> sport of it. (3)
All of them look <u>to</u> you (1)
to give them their food in <u>due</u> season. (2)
You give it to them; <u>they</u> gather it; (3)
you open your hand, and they are <u>filled</u> with good things. (4) *Refrain*

You hide your face, and they <u>are</u> terrified;
you take away their breath, and they die and return to <u>the</u> dust.
You send forth your Spirit, and they are <u>cre</u>ated;
and so you renew the face <u>of</u> the earth. *Refrain*

May the glory of the Lord endure <u>for</u> ever;
may the Lord rejoice in all <u>his</u> works.
He looks at the earth and <u>it</u> trembles;
he touches the mountains <u>and</u> they smoke. *Refrain*

I will sing to the Lord as long as <u>I</u> live;
I will praise the Lord while I have <u>my</u> being.
May these words of <u>mine</u> please him;
I will rejoice <u>in</u> the Lord. *Refrain*

Cantor sings refrain. All repeat refrain. Cantor sings verses. All sing refrain after each group of verses.
In the psalm-tone the singer leaves the reciting note on the underlined word or syllable.

PSALMS
55 You Are a Priest Forever

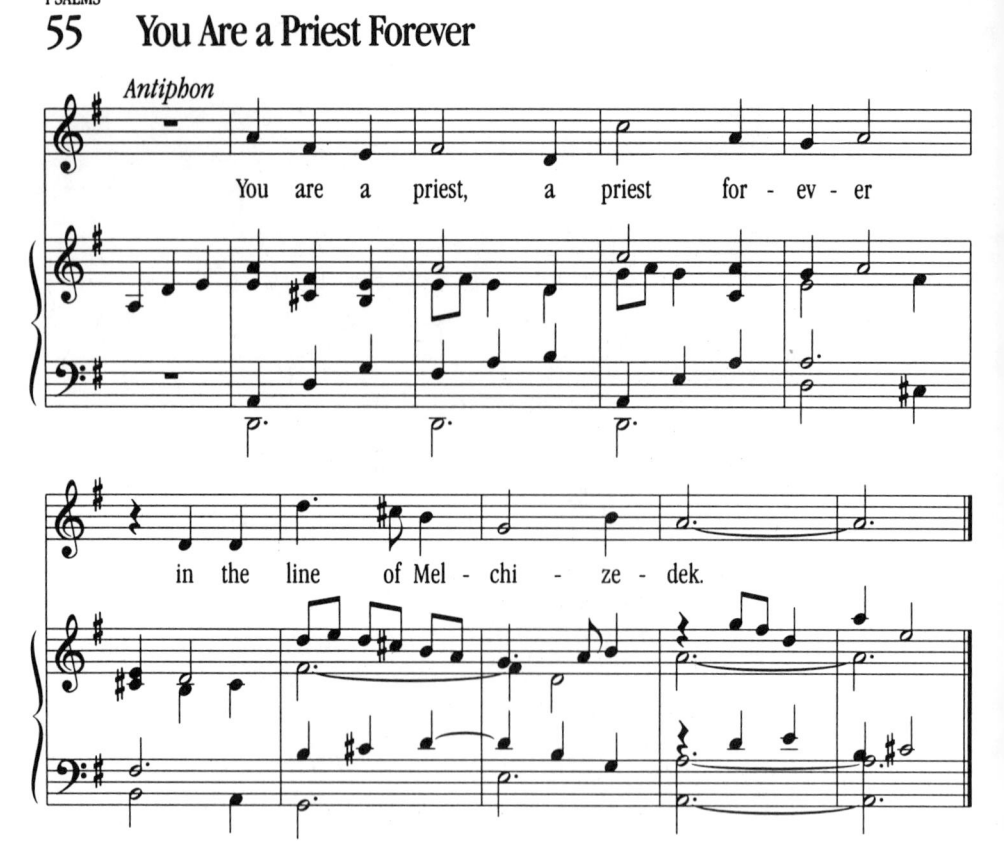

Antiphon

You are a priest, a priest for-ev-er in the line of Mel-chi-ze-dek.

Text: Psalm 110.
Music: Leo Nestor, 1986, 1989. © 1994, Selah Publishing Co., Inc. All rights reserved.

Verses

1 The Lord's reve-lation to my Master: "Sit on my right; your foes I will put be-neath your feet."
2 The Lord will wield from Zion your scep-ter of power; rule in the midst of all your foes.
3 A prince from the day of your birth on the ho-ly mountains; from the womb before the dawn I be-got you.
4 The Lord has sworn an oath he will not change. "You are a priest for ever, a priest like Mel-chize-dek of old."

PSALMS
56 On This Day the Lord Has Acted

Intonation

Refrain

On this day the Lord has act-ed; we will re-joice and be glad. Al-le-lu-ia, al-le-lu-ia, al-le-lu-ia.

Cantor sings refrain. All repeat refrain. Cantor sings verses. All sing refrain after each group of verses. The refrain is based on the hymn tune GELOBT SEI GOTT by Melchior Vulpius. It may be sung with or without the alleluias, or the alleluias may be sung without the antiphon.

In the psalm-tone the singer leaves the reciting note on the underlined word or syllable. The accompaniment does not synchronize with the voice except for the last note. The singer should feel free to ornament the last note.

Text: Psalm 118:14-24.
Music: George Black, 1986. © Anglican Book Centre. Used by permission.

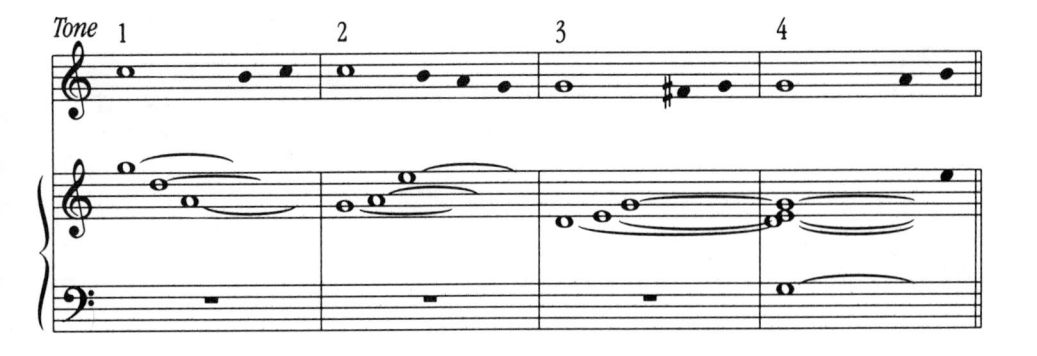

The Lord is my strength and <u>my</u> song, (1)
and he has become <u>my</u> salvation. (2)
There is a sound of exultation <u>and</u> victory (1)
in the tents <u>of</u> the righteousness: (2)
"The right hand of the Lord <u>has</u> triumphed! (3)
the right hand of the Lord is <u>ex</u>alted! (3)
the right hand of the Lord <u>has</u> triumphed!" (4) *Refrain*

I shall not die, <u>but</u> live,
and declare the works <u>of</u> the Lord.
The Lord has punished <u>me</u> sorely,
but he did not hand me over <u>to</u> death. *Refrain*

Open for me the gates of <u>righ</u>teousness;
I will enter them; I will offer thanks <u>to</u> the Lord.
"This is the gate of <u>the</u> Lord;
those who are righeous <u>may</u> enter." *Refrain*

I will give thanks to you, for <u>you</u> answered me
and have become <u>my</u> salvation.
The same stone which the builders <u>re</u>jected
has become the <u>chief</u> cornerstone. *Refrain*

This is the <u>Lord's</u> doing,
and it is marvelous <u>in</u> our eyes.
On this day the Lord <u>has</u> acted;
we will rejoice and <u>be</u> glad in it. *Refrain*

PSALMS
57 When the Lord Restored Our Fortunes

1 When the Lord restored our fortunes, we were like those who dream; our mouths were filled with laughter, our tongues with shouts of joy. We were like those who dream when the Lord, our

2 Lord, our God, restore our fortunes as you have watered the plain. May those who weep while sowing, return with shouts of joy, you have watered the plain.

3 When the Lord restores our fortunes, those who went forth in tears, who bore the seeds for sowing, will harvest sheaves of joy. Those who go forth in tears, when the

Text: Psalm 126; vers. Gracia Grindal, 1983.
Music: Donald Busarow, 1994.
Text and music © 1994, Selah Publishing Co., Inc. All rights reserved.

Irregular
IRONWOOD

G	F	C	G	C	Am7	G	

Lord re - stored our for - tunes; we were made glad!
God, re - store our for - tunes and make us glad!
Lord re - stores their for - tunes, will be made glad!

Give Thanks to the Lord

PSALMS 58

① *May be sung in canon* ② ③

1. Give thanks to the Lord, for he is good; his
2. Thank God who cre - a - ted even - ing's stars, whose
3. A God who with might - y out - stretched arm, whose
4. To God who re - mem - bers all our needs, whose

love en - dures for - ev - er. Give thanks to the Lord, the
love en - dures for - ev - er, who grant - ed the sun the
love en - dures for - ev - er de - liv - ered and blessed all
love en - dures for - ev - er, give thanks ev - er - more to

God of gods, whose love en - dures for - ev - er.
day - light hours, whose love en - dures for - ev - er.
Is - ra - el, whose love en - dures for - ev - er.
God our King, whose love en - dures for - ev - er.

Text: Psalm 136; para. Mark Sedio, 1984.
Music: Mark Sedio, 1984.
Text and music © 1994, Selah Publishing Co., Inc. All rights reserved.

97 97
ENDURING LOVE

PSALMS
59 In Deep Despair I Cry to You

1 In deep despair I cry to you—Lord, hear my voice, my prayer.
2 The sound-less whis-per of your voice, your hov-ering pres-ence near,
3 Be-cause your love is stead-fast, Lord, on you our hope re-lies;

If you should mark in-i-qui-ties, who would stand guilt-less there?
for these my long-ing spir-it waits as for the morn-ing clear,
you will re-deem your Is-ra-el from all in-i-qui-ties

But Lord, with you for-give-ness dwells and love be-yond com-pare.
as those who watch through-out the night till morn-ing shall ap-pear.
and turn to songs of thanks and praise our sor-row and our sighs.

Text: Psalm 130; para. Joy F. Patterson, 1991.
Music: *Sixteen Tune Settings*, 1812; attr. Elkanah Kelsey Dare; harm. David Ashley White, 1994.
Text and harm. © 1994, Selah Publishing Co., Inc. All rights reserved.

86 86 86
MORNING SONG

SCRIPTURAL SONGS
Ol' Noah Got Mad   60

Unison

1. Ol' No-ah got mad 'cause the rain kept a-drop-pin'.
2. He built him an ark 'cause the rain kept a-drop-pin'.
3. He float-ed the ark while the rain kept a-drop-pin'.
4. And when the rain stopped No-ah stopped all the mop-pin'.

Did-n't it rain? O did-n't it rain?

It rained for-ty days, for-ty nights with-out stop-pin'.
The an-i-mals came two by two with-out stop-pin'.
Un-til No-ah saw that the rain was a-stop-pin'.
The rain-bow ap-peared when the rain stopped a-drop-pin'.

Did-n't it rain? O did-n't it rain?

Text: Traditional; adapt. Barbara B. Bartlett, 1993. © 1994, Selah Publishing Co., Inc. All rights reserved.
Music: Traditional.

12 9 12 9
NOAH'S ARK

SCRIPTURAL SONGS
61 By Your Streams of Living Waters

1 By your streams of living waters, like a strong and fruitful tree,
  let me grow, Lord, in your knowledge and your faithful servant be.
  Night and day my meditation on your saving word shall stay;
  guide my thoughts, and all my living, in the straight and narrow way.

2 Let my life be rooted, grounded, in your love, O Christ my Lord;
  from the riches of your glory, strength of soul be my reward.
  Help me know your love's dimensions, boundless depth and width and height;
  come, Lord Jesus, dwell within me; with your fullness make me bright.

Text: Joy F. Patterson, 1990.
Music: *The Southern Harmony*, 1835; Margaret Mealy, 1980 (from *Songs for the People of God*).
Text and music © 1994, Selah Publishing Co., Inc. All rights reserved.

87 87 D
HOLY MANNA

SCRIPTURAL SONGS

Come, Satisfy Your Thirst 62

1. Come, satisfy your thirst with living waters! A royal feast is yours; come, eat your fill! Why labor for rewards that bring no lasting joy? God's food and drink eternally fulfill!

2. Of all his gifts, his presence is the greatest! Then seek the Lord, and you will surely find that in this banquet he is more than near to you— his life with yours is bound and intertwined!

Text: Isaiah 55:1-2; para. Keith Landis, 1987.
Music: Scottish melody; harm. Jeffrey Rickard, 1993 (from *Songs for the People of God*).
Text and harm. © 1994, Selah Publishing Co., Inc. All rights reserved.

11 10 12 10
KELVINGROVE

SCRIPTURAL SONGS

63 They Cast Their Nets in Galilee

1 They cast their nets in Gal-i-lee just off the hills of brown; such
2 Con-tent-ed, peace-ful fish-er-folk, be-fore they ev-er knew the
3 Young John who trimmed the flap-ping sail, home-less, in Pat-mos died. The
4 The peace of God, it is no peace, but strife closed in the sod. Yet

Text: William Alexander Percy, 1942, alt., ©. Used by permission of Leroy Pratt Percy.
Music: Betty Carr Pulkingham, 1972. © 1993, Selah Publishing Co., Inc. All rights reserved.

CM
FISHERFOLK

hap - py, sim - ple fish - er - folk, be - fore the Lord came
peace of God that filled their hearts brim - ful, and broke them,
ter, who hauled the teem-ing net, head - down was cru - ci -
let us pray for but one thing: the mar - velous peace of

down.
too.
fied.
God.

SCRIPTURAL SONGS
64 Our Father in Heaven

Unison

1. Our Father in heaven, we hallow your Name! Most holy and glorious, ever the same! Establish your kingdom, your purpose fulfill. On earth as in heaven, may all do your will!

2. Our daily bread give us, fulfil every need; grant food for both spirit and body, we plead. As we forgive others, our debts please forgive; with all reconciled and at peace may we live.

3. Then, from all temptation, come lead us away; from onslaught of evil, deliver we pray! For yours is the kingdom, the glory and power in past and in future, this day and this hour!

Text: *The Lord's Prayer* (Matthew 6:9-15); para. Keith Landis, 1986.
Music: Keith Landis, 1980; harm. John Rutter, 1980.
Text and music © 1994, Selah Publishing Co., Inc. All rights reserved.

11 11 11 11
PATTISON

SCRIPTURAL SONGS
Father in Heaven 65

1. Father in heaven we are truly your children; as children we approach you; as beloved children we call you by name: The power and glory are yours!

2. Your name be hallowed; by itself it is holy; now make it holy for us as your Word is taught to us: your Word is truth! The power and glory are yours!

3. Bring in your kingdom, though it comes in its own time. O let it come in our lives; as you give your Spirit, so we may believe. The power and glory are yours!

4. Your will be finished, here on earth as in heaven and help us do your bidding: curb the evil one, Lord, and keep us in faith. The power and glory are yours!

5. Give us bread daily, as you feed all your children.
O work thanksgiving in us
for your gifts which satisfy all of our needs:
The power and the glory are yours!

6. Forgive our sins as we forgive one another
O grant us grace to praise you
and to live in love for our friends and our foes:
The power and glory are yours!

7. Save us from trials so that even when tempted
we will not fall to sinning
into unbelief or to sins of despair:
The power and glory are yours!

8. Spare us from evil and from all that would harm us.
And when death comes to take us,
grant us life eternal and give us your peace.
The power and the glory are yours!

Text: *The Lord's Prayer* (Matthew 6:9-13, Luke 11:2-4); para. Gracia Grindal, 1987 (after Martin Luther).
Music: Mark Sedio, 1987.
Text and music © 1994, Selah Publishing Co., Inc. All rights reserved.

12 7 11 8
FATHER IN HEAVEN

SCRIPTURAL SONGS

66 Come to Me, O Weary Traveler

Unison

1. Come to me, O weary traveler; come to me with your distress; come to Me, you heavy-burdened; come to me and find your rest.
2. Do not fear, my yoke is easy; do not fear, my burden's light; do not fear the path before you; do not run from me in fright.
3. Take my yoke and leave your troubles; take my yoke and come with me. Take my yoke, I am beside you; take and learn humility.
4. Rest in me, O weary traveler; rest in me and do not fear. Rest in me, my heart is gentle; rest and cast away your care.

Text: Sylvia Dunstan (based on Matthew 11:28-30). © 1991, G.I.A. Publications. Used by permission.
Music: William P. Rowan, 1992. © 1993, Selah Publishing Co., Inc. All rights reserved.

87 87
AUSTIN

SCRIPTURAL SONGS
Myrrh-Bearing Mary   67

Unison

1 Myrrh-bearing Mary from Magdala came seeking her Jesus, with
2 Myrrh-bearing Mary to Bethany came seeking her Jesus who'd
3 Myrrh-bearing Mary to Calvary came seeking her Jesus who
4 Myrrh-bearing Mary to death's garden came seeking her Jesus who'd

spirit aflame. He had commanded her sickness depart;
called her by name; there she anointed his feet and his head
hung there in shame; and, as the careless and heedless passed by,
borne the world's blame; heart-sick, she stood, till she heard the Lord's voice:

she now would thank him for newness of heart.
with precious oils that were meant for the dead.
hopeless and helpless, she watched her Lord die.
"Mary!" he said, "I am risen; rejoice!"

In Eastern Churches, Mary Magdalene is known as one of the "Myrrh-bearing women" or "Myrrhophores" (Mark 16). Tradition has fused several women of the scriptures into Mary Magdalene.

Text: Rae E. Whitney, 1981. © 1990, Selah Publishing Co., Inc. All rights reserved.
Music: Alfred V. Fedak, 1989. © 1989, Selah Publishing Co., Inc. All rights reserved.

10 10 10 10
MYRRH-BEARING MARY

SCRIPTURAL SONGS
68 Myrrh-Bearing Mary

Unison

1. Myrrh-bearing Mary from Magdala came seeking her Jesus, with spirit aflame. He had commanded her sickness depart; she now would thank him for newness of heart.
2. Myrrh-bearing Mary to Bethany came seeking her Jesus who'd called her by name; there she anointed his feet and his head with precious oils that were meant for the dead.
3. Myrrh-bearing Mary to Calvary came seeking her Jesus who hung there in shame; and as the careless and heedless passed by, hopeless and helpless, she watched her Lord die.
4. Myrrh-bearing Mary to death's garden came seeking her Jesus who'd borne the world's blame; heart-sick, she stood, till she heard the Lord's voice: "Mary!" he said, "I am risen; rejoice!"

In Eastern Churches, Mary Magdalene is known as one of the "Myrrh-bearing women" or "Myrrhophores" (Mark 16). Tradition has fused several women of the scriptures into Mary Magdalene.

Text: Rae E. Whitney, 1981. © 1990, Selah Publishing Co., Inc. All rights reserved.
Music: Alec Wyton, 1993. © 1994, Selah Publishing Co., Inc. All rights reserved.

10 10 10 10
REJOICE

SCRIPTURAL SONGS
And Jesus Said 69

Unison

1 And Jesus said our God is like a shepherd who has lost a sheep, and leaving all the rest he searched until he found what had been lost. "Rejoice," he cried, "I've found the lost! Rejoice, rejoice with me, rejoice."

2 And Jesus said our God is like a woman who has lost a coin. She lit a lamp and searched all night until she found what had been lost. "Rejoice," she cried, "I've found the lost! Rejoice, rejoice with me, rejoice!"

3 And Jesus said our God is like a father who has lost a son. He waited every day for him until his son returned to him. "Rejoice," he cried, "my son came home! Rejoice, rejoice with me, rejoice!"

Text: Gracia Grindal, 1983.
Music: Joy F. Patterson, 1994.
Text and music © 1994, Selah Publishing Co., Inc. All rights reserved.

88 88 88
AND JESUS SAID

SCRIPTURAL SONGS

70 — When Jesus Entered Jericho

1. When Jesus entered Jericho a crowd soon gathered 'round
to see this mighty prophet whom they'd heard so much about;
and numbered there among them was one of modest frame,

2. With people standing everywhere, Zacchaeus could not see;
so running swiftly through the crowd, he climbed into a tree.
When Jesus came upon him, he shouted out his way:

3. Zacchaeus scrambled to the ground, excitement in his eye;
he welcomed Jesus heartily, and off they went to dine.
The people who had seen this were startled and surprised

4. Soon after dinner was complete Zacchaeus rose and said,
"If I have cheated anyone, I owe them now a debt:
one half of my possessions I'll give unto the poor,

5. And Jesus said, "Rejoice with me, a child of God is found!
Today salvation dwells here with the people of this house.
We join in celebration, regardless of all cost;

Text: Mark Sedio, 1985, based on Luke 19.
Music: Mark Sedio, 1985.
Text and music © 1994, Selah Publishing Co., Inc. All rights reserved.

Irregular
ZACCHAEUS

| G | | | C | D7 | G |

the wealth-y tax col - lec - tor chief, Zac - chae-us was his name.
"Zac-chae-us, come down in - stant-ly, I need a place to stay."
to think that Je - sus went and ate with some-one they despised.
and those whom I have tak - en from, I'll give back all times four!"
the Son of God has come to seek and save that which was lost."

| C | Am7 | Bm7 | Em7 | Am7 | A7 | D |

Zac - chae-us, Zac - chae-us, this one of mod-est frame,
Zac - chae-us, Zac - chae-us, he shout-ed out his way,
Zac - chae-us, Zac - chae-us, the peo-ple were sur-prised,
Zac - chae-us, Zac - chae-us, you're giv-ing to the poor?
Zac - chae-us, Zac - chae-us, be - lieve it, for it's true!

| G | E7 | Am7 | D7 | G |

the wealth-y tax col - lec - tor chief, Zac - chae-us was his name.
"Zac-chae-us, come down in - stant-ly, I need a place to stay."
to think that Je - sus went and ate with some-one they des-pised.
To those whom you have tak - en from you'll give back all times four?
The Son of God has come to save us all, in - clud-ing you!

SCRIPTURAL SONGS
71 They Have No Wine

Unison

1. "They have no wine," said Mary to Jesus Christ, her son; so seeing her compassion and love for everyone, he made new wine from
2. "We have no bread, dear Master," his friends said, in despair, "just these few loaves and fishes are all we have to share." But, when Christ blessed and
3. "We have no wine, Lord Jesus, nor have we any bread." "Dear children, with my Body and Blood your souls are fed; since in true hearts a-

Text: Rae E. Whitney, 1978.
Music: Wilbur Held, 1993.
Text and music © 1994, Selah Publishing Co., Inc. All rights reserved.

76 76 D
NEW WINE

wa - ter to grace that wed - ding hall, so
broke them, that of - fering mul - ti - plied, and
bid - ing my Spir - it longs to be— by

that they said in won - der, "This is the
Je - sus fed five thou - sand till all were
faith, and with thanks - giv - ing, come, take, and

best of all."
sat - is - fied.
feed on me!"

SCRIPTURAL SONGS

72 The Empty-Handed Fishermen

1. The empty-handed fishermen, their net fills when they cast again. Who shows abundance with a word? None dare to ask; it is the Lord.

2. There's breakfast waiting on the shore, with bread and fish upon a fire. Who stands and welcomes with a word? None dare to ask; it is the Lord.

3. Now as we gather in this place, our emptiness is touched by grace. Who counsels, welcomes, feeds, and more? Who dares to ask? It is the Lord!

Text: Richard Leach, 1987. © 1994, Selah Publishing Co., Inc. All rights reserved.
Music: Alfred V. Fedak, 1989. © 1989, Selah Publishing Co., Inc. All rights reserved.

LM
DAVENPORT

SCRIPTURAL SONGS

Not for Tongues of Heaven's Angels   73

1. Not for tongues of heav-en's an - gels, not for wis - dom to dis - cern, not for faith that mas - ters moun - tains, for this bet - ter gift we yearn:

2. Love is hum - ble; love is gen - tle; love is ten - der, true, and kind; love is gra - cious, ev - er pa - tient, gen - er - ous of heart and mind:

3. In the day this world is fad - ing faith and hope will play their part; but when Christ is seen in glo - ry, love shall reign in ev - ery heart:

4. Nev - er jeal - ous, nev - er self - ish, love will not re - joice in wrong; nev - er boast - ful nor re - sent - ful, love be - lieves and suf - fers long:

may love be ours, O Lord.

Text: I Corinthians 13; para. Timothy Dudley-Smith, 1984. © 1985, Hope Publishing Co., Carol Stream, IL 60188.
All rights reserved. Used by permission.
Music: Roy Hopp, 1988. © 1990, Selah Publishing Co., Inc. All rights reserved.

87 87 6
REINLYN

SCRIPTURAL SONGS
74 We Are Ambassadors for Christ

1. We are ambassadors for Christ, God appealing through us. We plead to all on his behalf: live your new life for God.
2. For us Christ came to share our sin, though against his nature, so that in him we might become the righteousness of God.
3. Christ died that we might live anew; our old selves are vanquished. He died for all, that we, through faith, might live our lives for him.
4. Accept this grace as given to you; now is your salvation. Be faithful servants with each day; serve him, then others, too.
5. We are ambassadors for Christ, God appealing through us. We plead to all on his behalf: live your new life for God.

after st. 4

Text: II Corinthians 5 & 6; para. Joel Martinson, 1986.
Music: Joel Martinson, 1986.
Text and music © 1994, Selah Publishing Co., Inc. All rights reserved.

CM
ANCHORAGE

SCRIPTURAL SONGS

Rejoice in Christ Jesus 75

1. Rejoice in Christ Jesus, in Jesus rejoice, and know that God is near. The time for gentleness has come. The time has come. Rejoice, the time has come.
2. Rejoice in Christ Jesus, in Jesus rejoice, there is no need to fear. The hour of anxiousness is gone. The hour is gone. Rejoice, the hour is gone.
3. Rejoice in Christ Jesus, in Jesus rejoice, sing praise to God in prayer. The day of thankful hearts is here. The day is here. Rejoice, the day is here.
4. Rejoice in Christ Jesus, in Jesus rejoice, the peace of God is near. The timeless peace will guard your mind. The peace is near. Rejoice, true peace is near.

Text: Rusty Edwards, 1993, based on Philippians 4:4-7.
Music: Wayne L. Wold, 1993.
Text and music © 1994 Selah Publishing Co., Inc. All rights reserved.

656 846
TRUE PEACE

CREATION AND PROVIDENCE

76 Before the Earth Was Tossed in Space

1 Before the earth was tossed in space, the light of heaven shone from your face;
  as you turned darkness into day, reveal your glory, Lord, we pray.

2 When Moses met with Israel's Lord on Sinai's peak, your brightness poured;
  as he in friendship talked with you, reveal your glory, Lord, anew!

3 Elijah heard that still small voice; to follow you became his choice;
  as you new power on him did pour, reveal your glory, Lord, once more!

4 A star shone forth upon the earth to guide those guests to greet your birth;
  as Wise Men saw the Child adored, reveal your glory, now, O Lord!

5 Your friends upon the Mount, who saw
  transfiguring Light, were filled with awe;
  as you shone for these chosen three,
  reveal your glory, Lord, to me!

6 Upon the cross, your light grew dim;
  they tortured you in every limb;
  but, conquering death, you rose to reign;
  reveal such glory, Lord, again!

Text: Rae E. Whitney, 1990.
Music: Joel Martinson, 1994.
Text and music © 1994, Selah Publishing Co., Inc. All rights reserved.

LM
HILLCREST

CREATION AND PROVIDENCE

God of Unknown, Distant Worlds

77

1. God of unknown, distant worlds, ruler of all time and space,
far above all human thought, mind beyond our power to trace—
teach us, God, to comprehend majesty which has no end.

2. Tender God who stoops to earth, nurturing us with parent's love,
guiding, teaching us to stand, freeing us to live and move—
teach us, God, to comprehend giving love which has no end.

3. God whose sheltering love surrounds all creation, near and far—
creature, human, atom, flower, galaxy and moon and star—
help us our own love extend like your love which has no end.

Text: Joy F. Patterson, 1991. © 1994, Selah Publishing Co., Inc. All rights reserved.
Music: Roy Hopp, 1990. © 1990, Selah Publishing Co., Inc. All rights reserved.

77 77 77
SISTER BAY

CREATION AND PROVIDENCE

78 Old Abraham Fell Down

1. Old Abraham fell down and laughed to hear that he would have a son, and Sarah laughed to hear the news that motherhood was soon to come.
2. Though Abraham and Sarah laughed, is anything too hard for God? "He laughs" is what they named the child, born in the spring, as God had said.
3. Come, Lord of laughter, make us laugh, with promises we can't believe, the new life we were longing for and knew that we could not conceive.
4. Come, Lord of laughter, make us laugh, at certainties you make untrue, with promises so wild and free, come laugh with us, we'll laugh with you.

Text: Richard Leach, 1989.
Music: Wayne L. Wold, 1994.
Text and music © 1994, Selah Publishing Co., Inc. All rights reserved.

LM
LAUGHTER

CREATION AND PROVIDENCE

Where You Are, There Is Life 79

1 Where you are, there is life: the cos-mic "Let there
2 Where you are, there is love: a prom-ise made and
3 Where you are, there is peace: a rest-ing place at
4 True life and love and peace you are, and we are

be!" the "La-za-rus, come forth!" With-out you noth-ing
kept, one Son who dies for all, a love that ban-ish-
last, no run-ning an-y-more, for-giv-en and for-
yours, Cre-a-tor, Lamb, and Dove. Make us par-tak-ers

is or grows, your Word um-bil-i-cal to all.
es all fear, that, like its Fath-er, nev-er ends.
giv-ing friends, the quest of all who share your plan.
of your dream; see what your heart and hands have done,

Where you are, there is life— and you are here!
Where you are, there is love— and you are here!
Where you are, there is peace— and you are here!
and smile and say a-gain: how good, how good!

Text: Jaroslav J. Vajda, 1987, ©. Used by permission.
Music: Mark Sedio. © 1994, Selah Publishing Co., Inc. All rights reserved.

666 88 64
ORAVA

CREATION AND PROVIDENCE

80 We Are Not Our Own

1. We are not our own. Earth forms us, human leaves on nature's growing vine,
2. We are not alone. Earth names us: past and present, peoples near and far,
3. Through a human life God finds us; dying, living, love is fully known,
4. Therefore let us make thanksgiving, and with justice, willing and aware,
5. And if love's encounters lead us on a way uncertain and unknown,
6. Let us be a house of welcome, living stone upholding living stone,

fruit of many generations,
family and friends and
and in bread and wine re-
give to earth, and all
all the saints with prayer sur-
gladly showing all our

Text: Brian Wren, 1987. © 1988, Hope Publishing Co., Carol Stream, IL 60188. All rights reserved. Used by permission.
Music: David Hurd, 1990. © 1994, Selah Publishing Co., Inc. All rights reserved.

89 85
NEXUS

a - tions,	seeds	of	life		di -	vine.
stran - gers	show	us	who		we	are.
minds us:	we	are	not		our	own.
liv - ing,	lit -	ur -	gies		of	care.
round us:	we	are	not		a -	lone.
neigh - bors		we	are	not	our	own!

CREATION AND PROVIDENCE

We Marvel at Your Mighty Deeds 81

1 We mar - vel at your migh - ty deeds, Lord God of time and space;
2 Who shall not pay you hom - age, Lord, and bless your sa - cred Name?

we praise your truth and righ - teous - ness, great King of bound - less grace:
Be - cause your just and ho - ly works your sov - ereign power pro - claim,

for through each won - der and de - cree your stead - fast love we trace.
all na - tions will at last draw near and you a - lone ac - claim.

Text: Revelation 15:3-4; para. Carl P. Daw, Jr., 1986. © 1989, Hope Publishing Co., Carol Stream, IL 60188.
All rights reserved. Used by permission.
Music: Roy Hopp, 1988. © 1990, Selah Publishing Co., Inc. All rights reserved.

86 86 86
BENTBROOK

CREATION AND PROVIDENCE

82   We Praise You, O God

1. We praise you, O God; we ac-knowl-edge you to be the Lord; all cre-a-tion wor-ships you; the an-gels cry a-loud to you; with heav-en and all its
2. The a-pos-tles u-nite as the fel-low-ship of proph-ets join voic-es prais-ing you, O God. The no-ble mar-tyrs praise your name; the Church through-out all the
3. O Fath-er of might, with your love-ly one and on-ly Son, Ho-ly Spir-it, Com-fort-er. You are the King of glo-ry, Christ, the Fath-er's e-ter-nal
4. We praise you, O Christ; you are seat-ed there at God's right hand. We be-lieve that you will come to be our Judge. We pray for help; re-store those who are your
5. We praise you, O Christ. Come de-liv-er us and make us yours, num-bered there a-mong the saints who sing your prais-es day and night. O Lord, save your peo-ple,

Text: *Te Deum Laudamus*; vers. Gracia Grindal, 1993.
Music: Mark Sedio, 1993.
    Text and music © 1994, Selah Publishing Co., Inc. All rights reserved.

PM
CHAPEL OF THE INCARNATION

pow - ers, with the Cher - u - bim and Ser - a - phim, they cry,
a - ges is ac - know - ledg - ing that you are God; they cry,
Son, who has de - liv - ered us by be - ing born of a
ser - vants, whom you have re - deemed by your dear blood, who cry,
bless them, keep us free from sin; have mer - cy, Lord. You are

"Ho - ly! Ho - ly! Ho - ly! Lord God of Sa - ba -
"Ho - ly! Ho - ly! Ho - ly! Lord God of Sa - ba -
wo - man, o - ver - com - ing death's sharp - ness and the
"Ho - ly! Ho - ly! Ho - ly! Lord God of Sa - ba -
Ho - ly! Ho - ly! Ho - ly! Lord God of Sa - ba -

oth, heaven and earth are full of your glo - ry."
oth, heaven and earth are full of your glo - ry."
grave, o - pening heaven to all your be - liev - ers.
oth, heaven and earth are full of your glo - ry."
oth, heaven and earth are full of your glo - ry.

CREATION AND PROVIDENCE

83 King of Glory, King of Peace

1. King of glory, King of peace, I will love thee;
   and that love may never cease, I will move thee.
2. Wherefore with my utmost art, I will sing thee;
   and the cream of all my heart I will bring thee.
3. Seven whole days, not one in seven, I will praise thee;
   in my heart, though not in heaven, I can raise thee.

Text: George Herbert, "Praise (II)," 1633.
Music: David Charles Walker, 1976. © 1993 Selah Publishing Co., Inc. All rights reserved.

74 74 D
GENERAL SEMINARY

Small it is in this poor sort to en-roll thee;

Thou hast grant-ed my re-quest, thou hast heard me;
Though my sins a-gainst me cried, thou didst clear me;
Small it is in this poor sort to en-roll thee;

ev'n e-ter-ni-ty's too short to ex-tol thee.

thou didst note my work-ing breast, thou hast spared me.
and a-lone, when they re-plied, thou didst hear me.
ev'n e-ter-ni-ty's too short to ex-tol thee.

CREATION AND PROVIDENCE

84 God Whose Love We Cannot Measure

1. God whose love we cannot measure, hear our song of thanks, we pray!
Who could ever count the blessings that surround us every day?
For you give us light in darkness; in our weakness make us strong;
by your peace and tender comfort turn our sorrow into song.

2. In our hearts we bless and praise you—you have borne our heavy load;
here we thank you for your goodness—we your people, you our God:
Father, Son, and Holy Spirit, Lord whose name we lift above,
you are Love from everlasting and to everlasting Love.

Text: Michael Perry, 1989, after St. Boniface (680-754). © 1989, Hope Publishing Co., Carol Stream, IL 60188.
All rights reserved. Used by permission.
Music: Roy Hopp, 1989. © 1990, Selah Publishing Co., Inc. All rights reserved.

87 87 D
SILVER CREEK

CREATION AND PROVIDENCE

Sing, My Soul, His Wondrous Love   85

1. Sing, my soul, his wondrous love, who, from yon bright throne above, ever watchful o'er our race, still to us extends his grace.
2. Heav'n and earth by him were made; all is by his scepter swayed; what are we that he should show so much love to us below?
3. God, the merciful and good, bought us with the Savior's blood, and, to make our safety sure, guides us by his Spirit pure.
4. Sing, my soul, adore his Name! Let his glory be thy theme: praise him till he calls thee home; trust his love for all to come.

Text: Anonymous, ca. 1800.
Music: David Ashley White, 1982. © 1994, Selah Publishing Co., Inc. All rights reserved.

77 77
JOSEPHINE

CREATION AND PROVIDENCE

86 Now Thank We All Our God

1 Now thank we all our God, with heart and hands and voices, who wondrous things has done, in whom this world rejoices; who, from our mothers' arms, hath blessed us on our

2 O may this bounteous God through all our life be near us, with ever joyful hearts and blessed peace to cheer us; and keep us in God's grace, and guide us when per-

3 All praise and thanks to God, who reigns in highest heaven, to Father and to Son and Spirit now be given. The one eternal God, whom heaven and earth a-

Text: Martin Rinkhart, 1636.
Music: Hal H. Hopson, 1993. © 1993, Selah Publishing Co., Inc. All rights reserved.

67 67 66 66
NOLAN

way with count-less gifts of love, and still is ours to-day.
plexed, and free us from all ills in this world and the next.
dore, the God who was, and is, and shall be ev-er-more.

CREATION AND PROVIDENCE

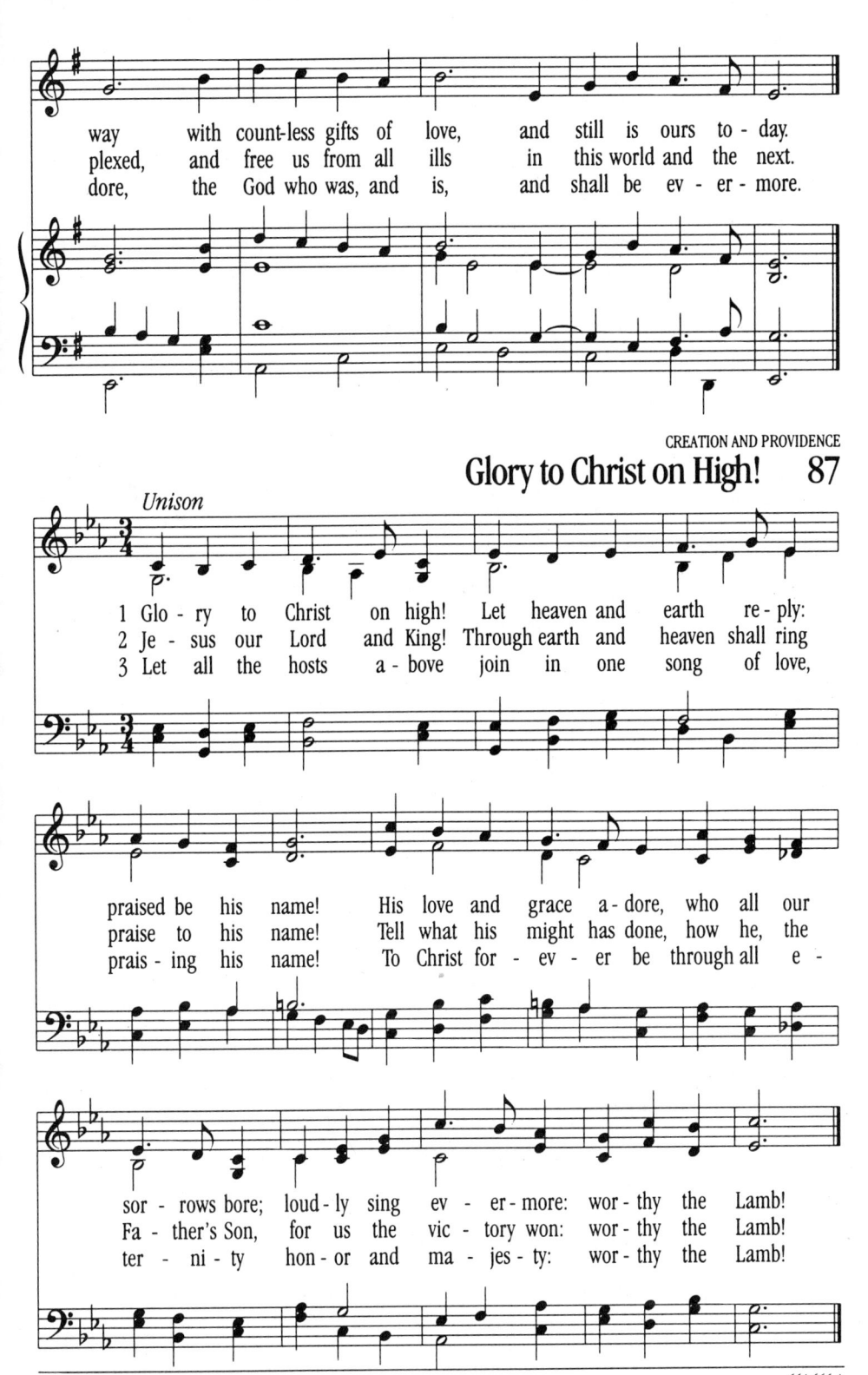

Glory to Christ on High! 87

Unison

1 Glo - ry to Christ on high! Let heaven and earth re - ply:
2 Je - sus our Lord and King! Through earth and heaven shall ring
3 Let all the hosts a - bove join in one song of love,

praised be his name! His love and grace a - dore, who all our
praise to his name! Tell what his might has done, how he, the
prais - ing his name! To Christ for - ev - er be through all e -

sor - rows bore; loud - ly sing ev - er - more: wor - thy the Lamb!
Fa - ther's Son, for us the vic - tory won: wor - thy the Lamb!
ter - ni - ty hon - or and ma - jes - ty: wor - thy the Lamb!

Text: James Allen, alt.
Music: Christopher Uehlein, 1993. © 1994, Selah Publishing Co., Inc. All rights reserved.

664 666 4
WESELY

CREATION AND PROVIDENCE

88 Praise the Living God Who Sings

1 Praise the living God who sings, pulsing through created things,
har-mon-iz-ing nature's arts, voicing hope in human hearts!
Alleluia! Alleluia! God's eternal anthem rings!
Alleluia! Alleluia! Tell the nations God still sings!

2 Christ was born, and angels sang till the realms of heaven rang!
Jesus, God's own song on earth, sang of pardon, love, rebirth.
Alleluia! Alleluia! Christ who rose gives life new wings!
Alleluia! Alleluia! Easter people, God still sings!

3 Rise to sing where there is wrong: "Truth and justice have a song;
let the burdened find release; grant them freedom, hope, and peace!"
Alleluia! Alleluia! Seek the joy that justice brings!
Alleluia! Alleluia! Share the message, God still sings!

4 Celebrate creation's God! Magnify redemption's Lord!
Praise the Spirit's power to bring understanding as we sing!
Alleluia! Alleluia! Wake the wood-winds, pipes, and strings!
Alleluia! Alleluia! Join the anthem, God still sings!

Text: David A. Robb, 1985. © 1994, Selah Publishing Co., Inc. All rights reserved.
Music: William P. Rowan, 1985. © 1993, Selah Publishing Co., Inc. All rights reserved.

77 77 77 with Alleluias
SMITH

CREATION AND PROVIDENCE

Onward, You Saints   89

Unison

1 Onward, you saints, in joyous celebration,
  come, join the song, our mighty God proclaim.
  Tell of his love, rejoice with jubilation,
  how from his throne above to earth he came.

2 O Lord of hosts, how lovely is your dwelling,
  wherein your saints, now gather in your name.
  From strength to strength through ages past here telling
  the wondrous story of your boundless grace.

3 Almighty God, our Sun and Shield victorious,
  blessed are they who put their trust in you.
  To those who dwell within your mansions glorious,
  uncounted blessings on them you bestow.

4 Praise to the Father, Son, and Spirit holy,
  sing to our Lord, all earth and heaven above.
  With angel choirs unite, tell of his glory;
  onward, you saints, abiding in God's love.

Text and music: Mark Sedio, 1985. © 1994, Selah Publishing Co., Inc. All rights reserved.
Text and music © 1994, Selah Publishing Co., Inc. All rights reserved.

11 10 11 10
GOD'S LOVE

REDEMPTION

90 O God Who Made Us in Your Likeness

1. O God who made us in your likeness and gave the world into our care, that we might rule and serve cre-
2. To bear your image gives us freedom to love, to reason, and to choose; yet we fall short of your in-
3. How did we lose our birthright blessing? Why do we live apart from God? What has un-webbed us from cre-
4. We have misused our godlike freedom, rebelled and followed our own schemes; in place of God we have in-
5. Where shall we turn when our ways fail us? We have no help but God alone. Teach us, O God, your truth; re-

Text: Carl P. Daw, Jr., 1994. © 1994, Hope Publishing Co., Carol Stream, IL 60188. All rights reserved. Used by permission.   98 98 with refrain
Music: Alfred V. Fedak, 1994. © 1994, Selah Publishing Co., Inc. All rights reserved.   IMAGO DEI CAZENOVIA

a - tion,   we come   be - fore you with this   prayer:
ten - tion   and our   cre - a - tive powers a - buse.
a - tion,   so that   we feel a - lone and   odd?
vent - ed   vain i -   dols spun from fears and   dreams.
claim us,   till in   our lives your will is   known.

Re - store in us your im - age,   O God.

REDEMPTION

91 Into Our Loneliness

1. Into our loneliness come now, dear Savior, bringing your loveliness to empty lives; for 'mid unruliness, hungering, and failure, each heart for saintliness secretly strives.

2. Into our worldliness bring deeper meaning, as we seek godliness to make us whole. Show us the costliness of our salvation, and let your holiness transform each soul!

Text: Rae E. Whitney, 1992.
Music: Alfred V. Fedak, 1993.
Text and music © 1994, Selah Publishing Co., Inc. All rights reserved.

65 64 D
LOVELINESS

REDEMPTION

Music and Incense 92

1. Music and incense, dancing and laughter, welcome each sinner now to love's feast; come to the party, clothed in the finest, freely provided for every guest!

2. Shame and discomfort, fear of rejection, horror of dying, panic and pain: these will be banished by Christ our Savior, for he in glory ever will reign.

3. So enter, singing, circled by angels, knowing Christ's kingdom none can destroy; greeted by loved ones eagerly waiting, come, pardoned people, into his joy!

Text: Rae E. Whitney, 1992.
Music: Ray W. Urwin, 1994.
Text and music © 1994, Selah Publishing Co., Inc. All rights reserved.

55 54 D
KIDDER

REDEMPTION

93 Hope Is the Harrowing

1. Hope is the har-row-ing, when prom-is-es have plowed the earth, bro-ken, turned the heav-y sod. Hope is the har-row-ing, to make soil wel-come seed.

2. Hope is the hun-ger-ing, when prom-is-es have sown the earth, scat-tered, hid the cost-ly seed. Hope is the hun-ger-ing, un-til the seed bears fruit.

3. Hope does the har-vest-ing, when prom-is-es have born their fruit, full of joy as fin-est wine. Hope does the har-vest-ing, what joy to taste and share!

4. God of the prom-is-es that plow the earth and plow the heart, turn-ing sod and sow-ing seed, God of the prom-is-es, let har-vest come with joy!

Text: Richard Leach, 1991.
Music: David Ashley White, 1994.
Text and music © 1994, Selah Publishing Co., Inc. All rights reserved.

687 66
KENNAN NEW

REDEMPTION
Mercy Rises Like a Mountain   94

1. Mercy rises like a mountain when the valley lies too low; mercy rises like a fountain when the rivers run too slow. God will raise all mercy high when the valleys are too dry.

2. Grace will circle global sighing when the body needs the strength. Grace will raise the weak and dying; grace will go to every length. God will circle all the pain; sin will die, and love will reign.

3. Peace will break the bond of prison with the power of its love. Death will know when it is risen from within, beneath, above. God sends peace upon the earth through the spirit of rebirth.

4. Life will seek the force of sunlight; leaves will find their chlorophyll. Darkness finds the stars and moonlight; worried heart will find its will. Resurrection knows no end; God is life that will transcend.

Text: Herbert Brokering, 1985.
Music: Walter L. Pelz, 1985.
Text and music © 1994, Selah Publishing Co., Inc. All rights reserved.

87 87 77
GOD'S LOVE

CHURCH AND MISSION

95 Taking Bread to Bless and Break

Unison

1. Tak-ing bread to bless and break it, shar-ing now what you first gave,
2. Risk-ing peace in place of con-flict, reach-ing out to form-er foes,
3. Seek-ing first each oth-er's wel-fare, com-fort-ing each oth-er's pain,
4. Car-ing for the sick and need-y, tak-ing sides with the op-pressed,

we, your peo-ple in the Spir-it, wait on you to feed and save;
we now ask to be made per-fect in that one-ness none yet knows;
we can wit-ness with-out fan-fare to the faith which you sus-tain;
we who are by na-ture greed-y find our-selves in shar-ing blessed;

make your Church, O Lord, in this place love's mem-or-i-al and sign.

5 Bearing witness to God's Kingdom,
   worshipping the servant King,
   we, baptized into his freedom,
   yearn that all might with us sing:
      make your Church, O Lord, in this place
      love's memorial and sign.

6 Praise the Father, Son, and Spirit,
   loving, saving, feeding still;
   we by grace shall life inherit
   and the world its hopes fulfill;
      make your Church, O Lord, in this place
      love's memorial and sign.

Text: Jeffery Rowthorn, 1976. © 1994, Hope Publishing Co., Carol Stream, IL 60188. All rights reserved. Used by permission.
Music: Leo Nestor, 1987. © 1994, Selah Publishing Co., Inc. All rights reserved.

87 87 87
CARLTON WAY

When Christians Shared Agape Meals

CHURCH AND MISSION
96

1. When Christians shared agape meals, O Lord, your Spirit came to bless and love the infant church, which gathered in your name and set each heart aflame!
2. We gather still for love events and celebrate with song the pilgrimage our parents made to keep our people strong— and we would join the throng!
3. We clothe our faith and hope with love to meet our neighbors' needs, and find that serving you through them transcends our human creeds, fulfilling faith with deeds!
4. We also bring our burdens here and share them as we feast; grant us, O Lord, the gifts and grace to be each other's priest through whom your love's released!
5. Keep us in caring fellowship, and help us to respond by living out the banquet feast united by a bond in this world and beyond!

Text: David A. Robb, 1985. © 1994, Selah Publishing Co., Inc. All rights reserved.
Music: William P. Rowan, 1986. © 1993, Selah Publishing Co., Inc. All rights reserved.

86 86 6
TIMOTHY SQUARE

CHURCH AND MISSION

97 We Who Preach a Church United

1 We who preach a Church united in baptism, faith, and word, show instead a Church divided— shattered cross and broken Lord. Each of us proclaims the

2 We perpetuate the anger, pettiness, and self-conceit that has marred our Christian history, made our witness incomplete. Schism parcelled out God's

3 Father, send your Holy Spirit to unite and purify this fragmented Church of Jesus, lest it in disunion die. When we truly are one

Text: Rae E. Whitney, 1986. © 1990, Selah Publishing Co., Inc. All rights reserved.
Music: *The Sacred Harp*, 1844, attr. to Benjamin F. White; harm. Alfred V. Fedak, 1994.
Harm. © 1994 Selah Publishing Co., Inc. All rights reserved.

87 87 D
BEACH SPRING

Bi - ble, drinks the cup and eats the bread, yet our deeds deny the one-ness of our Lord, the Church's head.
king - dom; dis - cord caused flocks to di - vide. Hurts re - sult - ed from in - dif - ference, her - e - sy was born of pride.
Bo - dy, as Christ prayed for us to be, then the world will find the Sav - ior through our love and u - ni - ty!

CHURCH AND MISSION

98   Bush by the Fire Illumed

1. Bush by the fire il-lumed burns but is not con-sumed. Mo-ses had
not pre-sumed to speak your name. Stand-ing on ho-ly ground,
we, too, have heard the sound; your call is strong, pro-found, sets us a-flame.

2. Sent forth by your com-mand in-to the prom-ised land, signs of your
might-y hand led night and day. Bap-tized in-to your name,
we, too, have seen the flame, your sav-ing grace we claim, walk in your way.

3. Wea-ry in wan-der-ing, thirst-ing and hun-ger-ing, your man-na,
nour-ish-ing, came from a-bove. By your life-giv-ing bread
we, too, are rich-ly fed. Christ, ris-en from the dead, feeds us in love.

4. How shall we sing your praise, wor-ship in right-ful ways? In these and
fu-ture days, will faith be found? Guide through the wil-der-ness,
com-fort our an-xious-ness, grant us more faith-ful-ness. Ho-ly the ground!

Text and music: Wayne L. Wold, 1993.
Text and music © 1994, Selah Publishing Co., Inc. All rights reserved.

66 64 D
PARAMOUNT

CHURCH AND MISSION

Terra Sancta, Holy Land 99

1 Terra Sancta, Holy Land, here we come, a pilgrim band,
walking where the Savior trod, singing praises to our God.
2 Nazareth, Jerusalem, Bethany, and Bethlehem,
cities crowned with history's fame, each to us a holy name.
3 Near the Garden's olive trees, Christ in prayer the pilgrim sees,
and the stones to our hearts say, Christ the King has passed this way.
4 Here Christ died for you and me: touch the Rock of Calvary!
At the empty tomb then sing praises to our Risen King!

Refrain
Terra Sancta, Holy Land, here we come, a pilgrim band!

Text: Rae E. Whitney, 1964, 1992.
Music: Joel Martinson, 1989.
Text and music © 1994, Selah Publishing Co., Inc. All rights reserved.

77 77 77
JOYFUL STEPS

CHRISTIAN LIFE

100 Lord, Make Us Servants

Unison

1. Lord, make us servants of your peace: where there is hate, may we sow love; where there is hurt, may we forgive; where there is strife, may we make one.
2. Where all is doubt, may we sow faith; where all is gloom, may we sow hope; where all is night, may we sow light; where all is tears, may we sow joy.
3. Jesus, our Lord, may we not seek to be consoled, but to console, nor look to understanding hearts, but look for hearts to understand.
4. May we not look for love's return, but seek to love unselfishly. For in our giving we receive, and in forgiving are forgiv'n.
5. Dying, we live and are reborn through death's dark night to endless day. Lord, make us servants of your peace, to wake at last in heaven's light.

Text: James Quinn, S.J., (after a prayer attr. Francis of Assisi), 1969, ©. Selah Publishing Co., Inc., U. S. agent.
Music: David Ashley White, 1983. © 1994, Selah Publishing Co., Inc. All rights reserved.

LM
ROCHESTER

CHRISTIAN LIFE
Lord, Make Us Servants 101

1. Lord, make us servants of your peace: where there is hate, may we sow love; where there is hurt, may we forgive; where there is strife, may we make one.

2. Where all is doubt, may we sow faith; where all is gloom, may we sow hope; where all is night, may we sow light; where all is tears, may we sow joy.

3. Jesus, our Lord, may we not seek to be consoled, but to console, nor look to understanding hearts, but look for hearts to understand.

4. May we not look for love's return, but seek to love unselfishly. For in our giving we receive, and in forgiving are forgiv'n.

5. Dying, we live and are reborn through death's dark night to endless day. Lord, make us servants of your peace, to wake at last in heaven's light.

Text: James Quinn, S.J. (after a prayer attr. Francis of Assisi), 1969, ©. Selah Publishing Co., Inc., U.S. agent.
Music: K. Lee Scott, 1994. © 1994, Selah Publishing Co., Inc. All rights reserved.

LM
YOUNG

CHRISTIAN LIFE
102 Lord, Make Us Saints

1. Lord, make us saints of Christ-ly sight to be your proph-ets for the right; grant vis-ioned cour-age to be-hold new truths which speak from words of old, to hear your pro-cla-ma-tion still and dare risk all to voice your will.

2. Lord, make us saints who tow-er tall in mor-al hon-es-ty toward all, who keep be-liefs and eth-ics one through what is thought and said and done, till faith and works, with love, com-pose the streams through which your jus-tice flows.

3. Lord, make us saints of rug-ged strength who care and serve to an-y length, who hon-or Love once sac-ri-ficed by treat-ing all as kin of Christ, who seek, through prayer and care-ful thought, to live the way our Mas-ter taught.

4. Lord, make us saints in ev-ery age whose "Acts" ex-tend the sac-red page of those em-pow-ered from a-bove for lives of self-ex-pend-ing love, who catch the flame, and then be-come new pil-grim lights in Chris-ten-dom.

Text: David A. Robb, 1981. © 1994, Selah Publishing Co., Inc. All rights reserved.
Music: John B. Dykes, 1861.

88 88 88
MELITA

CHRISTIAN LIFE
Grant Us Wisdom to Perceive You 103

1 Grant us wisdom to perceive you, heart a-
2 Grant us faithfulness in praying, strength to
3 Grant us diligence in doing, patience
4 Grant us courage to proclaim you; may our

wakened to receive you, minds alert to thoughts that
keep our souls from straying, sense to cease from dis-o-
when your truth pursuing, eager to receive re-
actions never shame you, but as Lord forever

grieve you, Holy Father, hear us.
beying, Holy Father, hear us.
newing, Holy Father, hear us.
name you; Holy Father, hear us.

Text: Rae E. Whitney, 1989 (based on a prayer of St. Benedict).
Music: Carol Doran, 1994.
Text and music © 1994, Selah Publishing Co., Inc. All rights reserved.

88 86
BENEDICT

CHRISTIAN LIFE
104 Teach Us, Good Lord, to Serve

1 Teach us, good Lord, to serve as you alone deserve;
to give, not count the cost; to fight, though wars be lost
and wounds be sore and deep; to toil, though sick for sleep;

2 to labor, and to ask no payment for our task,
since (knowing we fulfill your loving, holy will),
it is enough to serve as you alone deserve.

Text: Rae E. Whitney, 1978 (after a prayer of Ignatius of Loyola). © 1990, Selah Publishing Co., Inc. All rights reserved.
Music: Peter Cutts, 1994. © 1994, Hope Publishing Co. Carol Stream, IL 60188. All rights reserved. Used by permission.

66 66 66
HASSMAN

CHRISTIAN LIFE

O God in Whom All Life Begins 105

1. O God in whom all life be-gins, who births the seed to fruit,
2. U-nite in mu-tual min-is-try our minds and hands and hearts
3. Through tears and laugh-ter, grief and joy, en-large our trust and care;

be-stow your bless-ing on our lives; here let your love find root.
that we may have the grace to seek the power your peace im-parts.
so bind us in com-mu-ni-ty that we may risk and dare.

Bring forth in us the Spir-it's gifts of pa-tience, joy, and peace;
So let our va-ried gifts com-bine to glo-ri-fy your Name
Be with us when we ga-ther here to wor-ship, sing, and pray,

de-liv-er us from numb-ing fear, and grant our faith in-crease.
that in all things by word and deed we may your love pro-claim.
then send us forth in power and faith to live the words we say.

Text: Carl P. Daw, Jr., 1990. © 1990, Hope Publishing Co., Carol Stream, IL 60188. All rights reserved. Used by permission.
Music: Roy Hopp, 1990. © 1990, Selah Publishing Co., Inc. All rights reserved.

CMD
ACCORD

CHRISTIAN LIFE
106 O God of Spring and Summer Days

1. O God of spring and summer days, we seek your presence here;
   remember us who sing your praise as winter nights draw near.
   Throughout our lives we've loved your name and never cease to pray—

2. We early sought to do your will; we served you in our youth;
   when we are old we need you still, the Way, the Life, the Truth.
   The burning bush, your laws on stone, the fire that led by night,

3. O God, who gave the mercy seat where sins may be forgiven,
   give us your victory in defeat and lead our souls to heaven.
   O God of spring and summer days, of fall and winter, too,

Text: Rae E. Whitney, 1978.
Music: Alfred V. Fedak, 1990.
Text and music © 1990, Selah Publishing Co., Inc. All rights reserved.

CMD
BEACH HAVEN

convince us you are still the same to-day as yes-ter-day.
remind us, when we feel a-lone, your Word pro-vides our light.
though a-ging voic-es sing your praise, our hearts are ev-er new!

What Can I Ask in Your Name 107

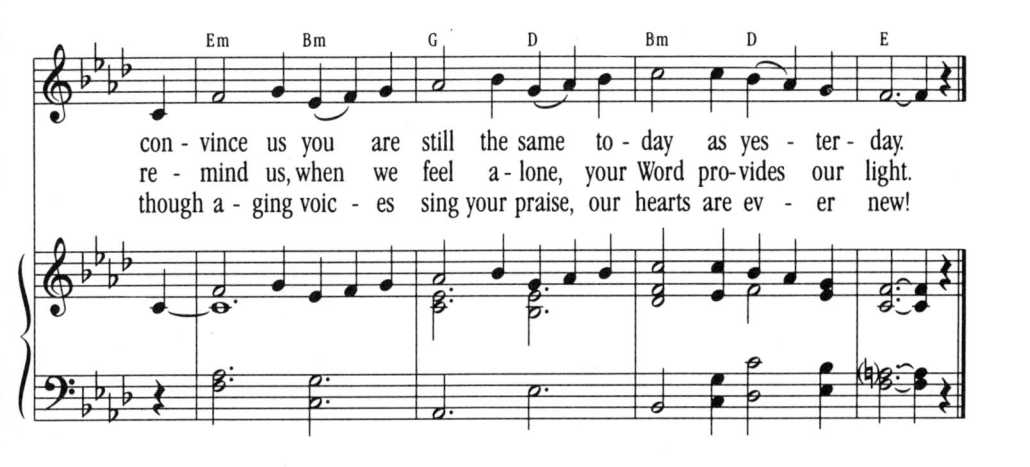

CHRISTIAN LIFE

1 What can I ask in your name? Noth-ing that caus-es you shame; and
2 What can I do in your name? Noth-ing that caus-es you shame; may
3 What can I give in your name? Noth-ing that caus-es you shame; I

I'll on-ly ask for help for my task, if it may your glo-ry pro-claim!
all that I do be of-fered to you that it may your glo-ry pro-claim!
pray, as I live, what-ev-er I give may al-ways your glo-ry pro-claim!

Text: Rae E. Whitney, 1991.
Music: Alec Wyton, 1994.
Text and music © 1994, Selah Publishing Co., Inc. All rights reserved.

77 55 8
GLORY

CHRISTIAN LIFE
108 The House of Faith

1. The house of faith has many rooms where we have never been;
there is more space within God's scope than we have ever seen.

2. We dare not limit God's domain to what our creeds declare,
or shrink from probing things unknown lest God should not be there.

3. The way to God is not escape, though truth does make us free:
the life of chosen servanthood is perfect liberty.

4. Yet still we seek at journey's end the last and sweetest grace:
the gift of room to turn around and know God face to face.

Text: Carl P. Daw, Jr., 1990. © 1990, Hope Publishing Co. Carol Stream IL 60188. All rights reserved. Used by permission.
Music: Iteke Prins, 1994. © 1994, Selah Publishing Co., Inc. All rights reserved.

CM
FAITH

CHRISTIAN LIFE
Light of the Minds That Know Him 109

1 Light of the minds that know him, may Christ be light to mine!
My sun in ris-en splen-dor, my light of truth di-vine,
my guide in doubt and dark-ness, my true and liv-ing way,
my clear light ev-er shin-ing, my dawn of heav-en's day.

2 Life of the souls that love him, may Christ be ours in-deed!
The liv-ing bread from heav-en on whom our spir-its feed,
who died for love of sin-ners to bear our guil-ty load
and make of life's brief jour-ney a new Em-ma-us road.

3 Strength of the wills that serve him, may Christ be strength to me,
who stilled the storm and tem-pest, who calmed the toss-ing sea;
his Spir-it's power to move me, his will to mas-ter mine,
his cross to car-ry dai-ly and con-quer in his sign.

4 May it be ours to know him that we may tru-ly love,
and lov-ing ful-ly serve him as serve the saints a-bove,
till in that home of glo-ry with fade-less splen-dor bright,
we serve in per-fect free-dom our Strength, our Life, our Light.

Text: Timothy Dudley-Smith (based on a prayer of Augustine of Hippo), 1976.
© 1984, Hope Publishing Co., Carol Stream, IL 60188. All rights reserved. Used by permission.
Music: Keith Landis, 1993; harm. Jeffrey Rickard, 1994. © 1994, Selah Publishing Co., Inc. All rights reserved.

76 76 D
CAVANAUGH

CHRISTIAN LIFE
110 Help Us Accept Each Other

1. Help us accept each other as Christ accepted us; teach us as sister, brother, each person to embrace. Be present, Lord, among us and bring us to believe we
2. Teach us, O Lord, your lessons, as in our daily life we struggle to be human and search for hope and faith. Teach us to care for people, for all— not just for some— to
3. Let your acceptance change us, so that we may be moved in living situations to do the truth in love; to practice your acceptance until we know by heart the
4. Lord, for today's encounters with all who are in need, who hunger for acceptance, for righteousness and bread, we need new eyes for seeing, new hands for holding on. Re-

Text: Fred Kaan, 1975. © 1975, Hope Publishing Co., Carol Stream, IL 60188. All rights reserved. Used by Permission.
Music: Roy Hopp, 1986. © 1990 Selah Publishing Co., Inc. All rights reserved.

76 76 D
OAKDALE

are our-selves ac - cept - ed   and meant to love and live.
love them as we find them   or as they may be - come.
ta - ble of for - give - ness   and laugh-ter's heal - ing art.
new us with your Spir - it,   Lord; free us, make us one!

Last time only

Help us ac-cept each oth - er   as Christ ____ ac - cept - ed us.
                                              ac-cept-ed

CHRISTIAN LIFE
May Peace Abide in Us 111

Unison

1 May peace a - bide in us   till that en - vi - sioned day when
2 May jus - tice live in us   till we walk in the light by
3 May love flow forth from us   till peo - ple share the bliss which

none shall fear or make a - fraid, and peace has come to stay.
which the just live out their faith, pur - su - ing truth and right.
draws the world in such em - brace that peace and jus - tice kiss.

Text: David A. Robb, 1985.
Music: *The Original Sacred Harp*, 1911; harm. Richard Hillert, 1980 (from *Songs for the People of God*).
Text and music © 1994, Selah Publishing Co., Inc. All rights reserved.

SM
TEACHER'S FAREWELL

CHRISTIAN LIFE
112 With Sounds of Gentle Stillness

1 With sounds of gentle stillness and quiet voice of calm,
by which you bring your bidding and sing your inner psalm,
inform our thoughts and motives by your internal voice,
and cultivate our conscience at every point of choice.

2 Keep every sense attentive; within our lives instill
the heartbeat of your presence, to know and do your will:
alert us to the needy, with hearts attuned to pain;
prepare our touch for comfort—our skills, for other's gain.

3 Forgive us when we fail you; reveal what we must mend;
renew your spirit in us that willful sin may end.
Lord, guide our thoughts and actions, advise us when we speak,
till private stillness strengthens the public walk we seek.

Text: David A. Robb, 1989.
Music: *The Southern Harmony*, 1835; harm. Margaret Mealy, 1977 (from *Songs for the People of God*).
Text and harm. © 1994, Selah Publishing Co., Inc. All rights reserved.

76 76 D
COMPLAINER

CHRISTIAN LIFE
Give with Simplicity 113

1 Give with simplicity; give with humility;
  give with true-heartedness, for that is right.
  And then when others do some loving deed for you,
  thank them with gracefulness, share their delight!

2 Bless those who wish you harm; bless those who cause alarm;
  bless those who curse your name with words untrue.
  Since Jesus taught and stood for all things wise and good,
  yet bore abuse and blame, Christians must too.

3 Praise God with heart and soul; praise God who makes you whole;
  praise God for truth and love seen in his Son,
  for, as we live our creed, caring for those in need,
  with all the saints above Christ makes us one.

Text: Rae E. Whitney, 1991.
Music: Alec Wyton, 1993.
Text and music © 1994, Selah Publishing Co., Inc. All rights reserved.

666 4 D
WHITNEY

CHRISTIAN LIFE
114 Christ Be Beside Me

1. Christ be beside me, Christ be before me, Christ be behind me, king of my heart. Christ be within me, Christ be below me, Christ be above me, never to part.
2. Christ on my right hand, Christ on my left hand, Christ all around me, shield in the strife. Christ in my sleeping, Christ in my sitting, Christ in my rising, light of my heart.
3. Christ be in all hearts thinking about me, Christ be on all tongues telling of me. Christ be the vision in eyes that see me, in ears that hear me Christ ever be.

Text: James Quinn, S.J., 1969, ©. Selah Publishing Co., Inc., U.S. agent.
Music: Peter Cutts, 1986. © 1994, Hope Publishing Co., Carol Stream, IL 60188. All rights reserved. Used by permission.

555 4 D
MANY MANSIONS

Alternate harmonization

CHRISTIAN LIFE
Were the World to End Tomorrow 115

1 Were the world to end to-mor-row, would we plant a tree to-day?
2 Dare we try to give an an-swer, reach-ing out in frag-ile hope;
3 Born in-to the brit-tle morn-ing of that fi-nal earth-y day,
4 Pray that at the end of liv-ing, of phi-los-o-phies and creeds,

Would we till the soil of lov-ing, kneel to work and rise to pray?
touch-ing lives with words of Eas-ter, break a loaf and share a cup?
we would be in-tent on see-ing Christ in oth-ers on our way.
God will find his peo-ple bus-y plant-ing trees and sow-ing seeds.

Text: Fred Kaan, 1986. © 1989, Hope Publishing Co., Carol Stream, IL 60188. All rights reserved. Used by permission.
Music: Roy Hopp, 1990. © 1990, Selah Publishing Co., Inc. All rights reserved.

87 87
ARBOR DAY

CHRISTIAN LIFE

116 Lord, Make Me an Alleluia

May be sung in canon

1 Lord, make me an alleluia; Lord, make me an alleluia; Lord, make me an alleluia, from head to toe!
2 Lord, make me a faithful servant; Lord, make me a faithful servant; Lord, make me a faithful servant, from head to toe!
3 Lord, make me a friend to others; Lord, make me a friend to others; Lord, make me a friend to others, from head to toe!

4 Lord, make me a true believer...   5 Lord, make me a good disciple...

(Other stanzas are possible. Actions may also be invented,
ending with the obvious "from head to toe!")

Text: Rae E. Whitney (based on words of Augustine of Hippo), 1987.
Music: Ray W. Urwin, 1994.
Text and music © 1994, Selah Publishing Co., Inc. All rights reserved.

88 85
ALLELUIA ME FACE

Handbell or Orff inst. ostinati

CHRISTIAN LIFE

Lord, Make Me an Alleluia 117

1 Lord, make me an al-le-lu-ia; Lord, make me an al-le-lu-ia;
2 Lord, make me a faith-ful ser-vant; Lord, make me a faith-ful ser-vant;
3 Lord, make me a friend to oth-ers; Lord, make me a friend to oth-ers;

Lord, make me an al-le-lu-ia, from head to toe!
Lord, make me a faith-ful ser-vant, from head to toe!
Lord, make me a friend to oth-ers, from head to toe!

4 Lord, make me a true believer...
5 Lord, make me a good disciple...

(Other stanzas are possible. Actions may also be invented, ending with the obvious "from head to toe!")

Text: Rae E. Whitney (based on words of Augustine of Hippo), 1987. © 1994, Selah Publishing Co., Inc. All rights reserved.
Music: Peter Cutts, 1994. © 1994, Hope Publishing Co., Carol Stream, IL 60188. All rights reserved. Used by permission.

88 84
MINTON

CHRISTIAN LIFE
118 Lord, Glorify Yourself Today

Unison

1. Lord, glorify yourself today in all I think or do or say. From my first waking moment till each conscious thought in sleep lies still.
2. Then do not let your presence cease, but, in my dreams, your role increase! In each adventure, side by side, be my Companion, Friend, and Guide!

Text: Keith Landis, 1986.
Music: *The Southern Harmony*, 1835; harm. by Jack Noble White, 1982 (from *Songs for the People of God*).
Text and harm. © 1994, Selah Publishing Co., Inc. All rights reserved.

LM
PROSPECT

CHRISTIAN LIFE
There a Friend Is Weeping 119

Unison

1. There a friend is weeping, someone must be sad;
   when folk are unhappy who will make them glad?
2. There a flower is blooming bringing hope and joy;
   who will share its beauty with some girl or boy?
3. There a tune is sounding sweetly in each ear;
   who will sing it loudly for a friend to hear?
4. There a meal is cooking; what a lovely smell!
   Who will let another taste the food as well?

Refrain
Here am I! Here am I! Here am I! O send me, Lord!

5. There some folk are dancing
   through a city's street;
   who will teach such rhythm
   to another's feet? *Refrain*

6. There are people painting
   colors, movement, light;
   who will help the pictures
   make a dark room bright? *Refrain*

7. There are many lonely—
   life seems so unfair:
   who will smile and greet them,
   show them that we care? *Refrain*

Text: Rae E. Whitney, 1989.
Music: Amanda Husberg, 1994.
Text and music © 1994, Selah Publishing Co., Inc. All rights reserved.

65 65 and refrain
HERE AM I

CHRISTIAN LIFE
120 Heirs Together of God's Grace

1 Heirs together of God's grace, sons and daughters, dearly loved, chosen not for gender, race, achievements, or ability, we marvel at our honored place in God's adopted family.

2 Called as partners to one task, privileged to help unmask creation's God on history's stage; to take the selfless role of love, our lives revealing Jesus' face and drawing others to God's grace.

3 Called to clothe ourselves with Christ, bearing scars of sacrifice; our broken bodies, broken lives are held and healed in his embrace: a holy people clothed in traits of kindness and humility.

4 Gifted with diversity, all our curious melodies together blend in harmony, creating one majestic song that fills and floods created space with rich and wondrous sounds of praise.

Text and music: AnnaMae Meyer Bush, 1990.
Text and music © 1994, Selah Publishing Co., Inc. All rights reserved.

Irregular
VAN HAMERSVELD

CHRISTIAN LIFE

Surely It Is God Who Saves Me   121

1. Surely it is God who saves me; I shall trust and have no fear.
For the Lord defends and shields me and his saving help is near.
So rejoice as you draw water from salvation's healing spring;
in the day of your deliverance thank the Lord, his mercies sing.

2. Make God's deeds known to the peoples: tell out his exalted Name.
Praise the Lord, who has done great things; all his works God's might proclaim.
Zion, lift your voice in singing; for with you has come to dwell
in your very midst the great and Holy One of Israel.

Text: *The First Song of Isaiah* (Isaiah 12:2-6); para. Carl P. Daw, Jr., 1982.
© 1982, Hope Publishing Co., Carol Stream, IL 60188. All rights reserved. Used by permission.
Music: Alfred V. Fedak, 1990. © 1990 Selah Publishing Co., Inc. All rights reserved.

87 87 D
Ecce, Deus

CHRISTIAN LIFE
122 Surely It Is God Who Saves Me

1 Sure - ly it is God who saves me; I shall trust and have no fear.
2 Make God's deeds known to the peo - ples: tell out his ex - alt - ed Name.

For the Lord de - fends and shields me and his sav - ing help is near.
Praise the Lord, who has done great things; all his works God's might pro - claim.

So re - joice as you draw wa - ter from sal - va - tion's heal - ing spring;
Zi - on, lift your voice in sing - ing; for with you has come to dwell

Text: *The First Song of Isaiah* (Isaiah 12:2-6); para. Carl P. Daw, Jr., 1982. © 1982, Hope Publishing Co., Carol Stream, IL 60188.
All rights reserved. Used by permission.
Music: David Hurd, 1985. © 1994, Selah Publishing Co., Inc. All rights reserved.

87 87 D
SURELY IT IS GOD

in the day of your de-liv-erance thank the Lord, his mer-cies sing.
in your ve-ry midst the great and Ho-ly One of Is-ra-el.

CHRISTIAN LIFE
Day by Day 123

Unison

Day by day, dear Lord, of thee three things I pray: to see thee more clear-ly, love thee more dear-ly, fol-low thee more near-ly, day by day.

Text: Attr. Richard of Chichester, 13th cent.
Music: Keith Landis, 1993; harm. Alfred V. Fedak, 1993. © 1994, Selah Publishing Co., Inc. All rights reserved.

Irregular
DAY BY DAY

CHRISTIAN LIFE
124 Love Is of God

1. Love is of God; in love his love is known; in those who love the love of God is shown.
2. Joy is of God, in whom all joy is found; in Christ our joy the joys of heav'n abound.
3. Peace is of God; like gentlest dew he sends his peace on those whom love has made his friends.
4. Light is of God; whoever walks in light has Christ beside to guide through darkest night.
5. Glory is theirs in whom the Spirit dwells, whose light all light, whose love all love excels.
6. Love is of God; in love his love is known; in those who love the love of God is shown.

Text: James Quinn, S.J., 1969, ©. Selah Publishing Co., Inc., U.S. agent.
Music: Alfred V. Fedak, 1994. © 1994, Selah Publishing Co., Inc. All rights reserved.

10 10
QUINN

CHRISTIAN LIFE

O Jesus, I Have Promised   125

Unison

1. O Jesus, I have promised to serve thee to the end.
   Be thou forever near me, my Master and my Friend.
   I shall not fear the battle, if thou are by my side,
   nor wander from the pathway, if thou wilt be my guide.

2. O let me feel thee near me; the world is ever near.
   I see the sights that dazzle; the tempting sounds I hear.
   My foes are ever near me, around me and within,
   but, Jesus, draw thou nearer, and shield my soul from sin.

3. O let me hear thee speaking in accents clear and still,
   above the storms of passion, the murmurs of self-will.
   O speak to reassure me, to hasten or control,
   O speak, and make me listen, thou Guardian of my soul.

4. O Jesus, thou hast promised to all who follow thee
   that where thou art in glory there shall thy servant be.
   And, Jesus, I have promised to serve thee to the end.
   O give me grace to follow, my Master and my Friend.

Text: John Ernest Bode, 1868; *SPCK Psalms and Hymns, Appendix*, 1869.
Music: David Ashley White, 1983. © 1991 Selah Publishing Co., Inc. All rights reserved.

76 76 D
HOMAGE

MYSTERY OF GOD
126 Come, My Way, My Truth, My Life

1 Come, my Way, my Truth, my Life: such a Way as gives us breath; such a Truth as ends all strife; such a Life as kill-eth death.

2 Come, my Light, my Feast, my Strength: such a Light as shows a feast; such a Feast as mends in length; such a Strength as makes his guest.

3 Come, my Joy, my Love, my Heart: such a Joy as none can move; such a Love as none can part; such a Heart as joys in love.

Text: George Herbert, "The Call," 1633.
Music: Joel Martinson, 1992. © 1994, Selah Publishing Co., Inc. All rights reserved.

77 77
KESSLER PARK

MYSTERY OF GOD
Without the Fire 127

1. With-out the Fire, there is no Burn-ing; with-out the Teach-er, there's no Learn-ing; with-out the Shep-herd, no safe Keep-ing; with-out the Sow-er, there's no Reap-ing.
2. With-out the Judge, there is no Plead-ing; with-out the Bread, no heav'n-ly Feed-ing; with-out the Vine, no ho-ly Drink-ing; with-out the Mind, no Christ-ly Think-ing.
3. With-out the Way, there is no Go-ing; with-out the Truth, no in-ward Know-ing; with-out the Life, there is no Liv-ing; with-out the Cross, no full For-giv-ing.
4. With-out the Grave, no Res-ur-rect-ing; with-out the Light, no Love's Re-flect-ing; with-out the Vi-sion, no clear Dream-ing; with-out the Sav-ior, no Re-deem-ing.

Text: Rae E. Whitney (based on three lines by Thomas à Kempis), 1987. © 1991, Selah Publishing Co., Inc. All rights reserved.
Music: David Ashley White, 1992. © 1994, Selah Publishing Co., Inc. All rights reserved.

99 99
CONWAY

MYSTERY OF GOD
128 Wondrous God, More Named Than Known

1. Wondrous God, more named than known, give us, firm and certain grown, grace to doubt what we surmise, lest we miss the glad surprise when we find your truth exceeds all the forecasts of our creeds.

2. Pregnant Silence, lively Calm, Singer of creation's psalm, great "I AM" of burning bush: still resist our urge to push till you fit the names we choose, shadows of the light we lose.

3. Save us from proud, empty claims in our zeal to give you names. Let our notions be expressed not to limit but suggest views that icon-like disclose splendor more than we suppose.

4. God not female, God not male, God for whom all labels fail, Truth beyond our verbal games, Life too vast to bound with names: from vain word-lust set us free to embrace your mystery.

Text: Carl P. Daw, Jr., 1989. © 1990, Hope Publishing Co., Carol Stream, IL 60188. All rights reserved. Used by permission.
Music: Roy Hopp, 1990. © 1990, Selah Publishing Co., Inc. All rights reserved.

77 77 77
SISTER BAY

MYSTERY OF GOD
Guided by God's Holy Grace 129

1. Guided by God's holy grace we are held in one embrace.
  Neither death nor raging sea, nor the might of enemy
  will o'er-power the love and grace poured upon the human race.

2. Guided by God's grace alone, over desert, mountain stone,
  miracles on every side, endless chasms, deep and wide;
  ah, the wonder and delight: Christ is guide, and Christ is light.

3. God has sent a steadfast love, cloud around and fire above,
  broken every fear and sword by the water and the word.
  We are guided to this place by salvation of God's grace.

4. Cloud by day and fire by night, wilderness to left and right,
  rescued from a sea of death, God gives daily life and breath;
  oh, the wonder in this place, bread and water full of grace.

5. One the praise and one the Lord,
  one salvation, one adored;
  one the grace and one the love,
  one the Spirit, one the dove;
  one the circle, one the sign,
  one the Savior, Son divine.

6. Generations sleep and rise,
  every day is God's surprise.
  First the dawn and then the night,
  then the deep and then the light.
  Oh, the wonder of the way
  grace will turn the night to day.

Text: Herbert Brokering, 1984.
Music: Walter L. Pelz, 1984.
Text and music © 1994, Selah Publishing Co., Inc. All rights reserved.

77 77 77
WICHITA

MYSTERY OF GOD
130 Of Women and of Women's Hopes

1 Of women and of women's hopes we sing: of sharing in creation's
nurturing, of bearing and of birthing new belief, of
passion for the promises of life.

2 We praise the God whose image is our own, the mystery within our
flesh and bone, the woman-spirit moving through all time in
prophecy, Magnificat, and dream.

3 We labor for the commonwealth of God and, equal as disciples,
walk the road, in work and status, asking what is just, for
sisters of the family of Christ.

4 Forgiving what is past, we seek the new: a finer justice and a
peace more true, the promise of empowering for our day when
men and women roll the stone away.

Text: Shirley Erena Murray, 1992. © 1992, Hope Publishing Co., Carol Stream, IL 60188. All rights reserved. Used by permission. 10 10 10 10
Music: Kevin Hackett, 1993. © 1994, Selah Publishing Co., Inc. All rights reserved. HOBBS

MYSTERY OF GOD

God of Grace and God of Laughter   131

1 God of grace and God of laugh-ter, sing-ing worlds from nought to be—
2 When our lives are torn by sad-ness, heal our wounds with tune-ful balm;
3 Turn our sigh-ing in-to sing-ing, mu-sic born of hope re-stored;

sun and stars and all there-af-ter joined in cos-mic har-mo-ny:
when all seems dis-cord-ant mad-ness, help us find a mea-sured calm.
set our souls and voic-es ring-ing, tune our hearts in true ac-cord:

give us songs of joy and won-der, mu-sic mak-ing hearts re-joice;
Stead-y us with mu-sic's an-chor when the storms of life in-crease;
till we form a might-y cho-rus join-ing an-gel choirs a-bove,

let our prais-es swell like thun-der, ech-o-ing our Mak-er's voice.
in the midst of hurt and ran-cor, make us in-stru-ments of peace.
with all those who went be-fore us, in e-ter-nal hymns of love.

Text: Carl P. Daw, Jr., 1989. © 1989, Hope Publishing Co., Carol Stream, IL 60188. All rights reserved. Used by permission.
Music: Roy Hopp, 1990. © 1990, Selah Publishing Co., Inc. All rights reserved.

87 87 D
ISAAC

MYSTERY OF GOD

132 O God, on Whom We Lost Our Hold

1. O God, on whom we lost our hold when all your names were changed,
we find our prayers and hymns confused, more awkward and estranged.
Yet there is hope in these new words, sweet fruit in bitter rind:

2. The language which we knew so well flowed smoothly on the tongue,
though seldom did we pause to weigh how things were said or sung.
But now the world is showing us with stunning clarity

3. Dear God, inspire our hearts and minds to seek your truth anew,
and help us with each fresh insight to find names fit for you.
Yet never let us idolize the images we choose;

Text: Carl P. Daw, Jr., 1989. © 1990, Hope Publishing Co., Carol Stream, IL 60188. All rights reserved. Used by permission.
Music: Alfred V. Fedak, 1990. © 1990, Selah Publishing Co., Inc. All rights reserved.

CMD
PETER'S BROOK

the prom-ise of a keen-er faith than that we leave be-hind.
the prob-lems with the words we used to tame a mys-ter-y.
but as we strive, give us the grace to wres-tle and to lose.

NEW HEAVEN AND EARTH
God's Judgment Comes Like Fire 133

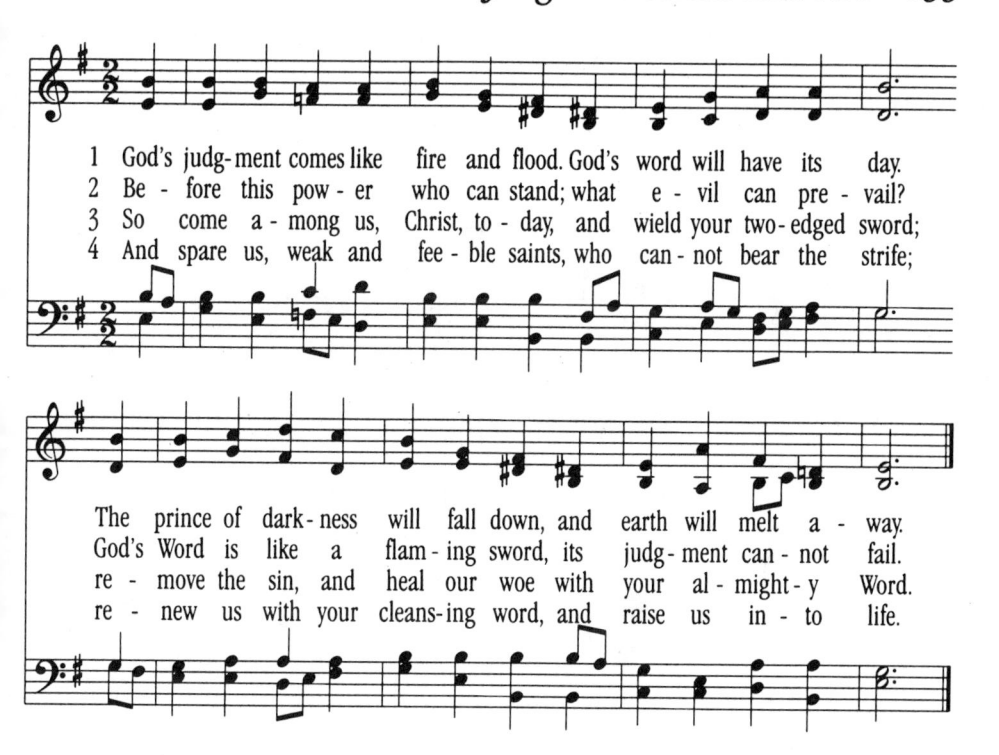

1 God's judg-ment comes like fire and flood. God's word will have its day.
2 Be-fore this pow-er who can stand; what e-vil can pre-vail?
3 So come a-mong us, Christ, to-day, and wield your two-edged sword;
4 And spare us, weak and fee-ble saints, who can-not bear the strife;

The prince of dark-ness will fall down, and earth will melt a-way.
God's Word is like a flam-ing sword, its judg-ment can-not fail.
re-move the sin, and heal our woe with your al-might-y Word.
re-new us with your cleans-ing word, and raise us in-to life.

Text: Gracia Grindal, 1992.
Music: David Ashley White, 1981.
Text and music © 1994 Selah Publishing Co., Inc. All rights reserved.

CM
NASHUA

NEW HEAVEN AND EARTH
134 Rejoice, the Lord Is King!

1 Rejoice, the Lord is King! Your Lord and King adore!
2 The Lord the Savior reigns, the God of truth and love:
3 His kingdom cannot fail; he rules o'er earth and heaven;
4 Rejoice in glorious hope! Our Lord the Judge shall come

Mortals, give thanks and sing, and triumph evermore.
when he had purged our stains, he took his seat above.
the keys of death and hell to Christ the Lord are given.
and take his servants up to their eternal home.

Refrain
Lift up your heart! lift up your voice! and once again I say, rejoice!

Text: Charles Wesley, 1744, alt.
Music: Keith Landis, 1986; harm Jeffrey Rickard, 1986. © 1994, Selah Publishing Co., Inc. All rights reserved.

66 66 88
MIDNIGHT CRY

NEW HEAVEN AND EARTH
Sorrow and Gladness 135

1 Sor-row and glad-ness are sis-ter and bro-ther; for-tune, mis-for-tune, both stand side by side. Gain and ad-vers-i-ty fol-low each oth-er; sun-shine makes sha-dows, and there e-vil hides. Gold has no worth af-ter our death; lay up your trea-sures in heav-en, not earth.

2 Love-li-est ros-es grow out of the bri-ar; beau-ti-ful flow-ers grow dead-li-est fruit. Un-der the laugh-ter the heart may be cry-ing; un-der the joy may be grief at the root. Deep in the rose e-vil may grow. On-ly in heav-en is life free from woe.

3 There will my sor-row and suf-fering be end-ed; there will God grant me a crown and re-ward. There will I sing and my spir-it be tend-ed in the sweet man-sions pre-pared by my Lord. Sor-row will die un-der God's eye. Heav-en will blos-som like ros-es on high.

Text: Thomas H. Kingo, 1681; tr. Gracia Grindal, 1983.
Music: Carol Doran, 1994.
Text and music © 1994, Selah Publishing Co., Inc. All rights reserved.

11 10 11 10 44 10
KINGO

SOCIETY/SOCIAL CONCERNS

136 When Broken Is Normal

1 When broken is normal we need a new world—where wholeness is
normal and truth is no shock, where peace is no miracle,
love no surprise, where joy and not mourning brings tears to our eyes.

2 When broken is normal we need the whole truth, not half-truth half
hiding our world and ourselves, not minds and hearts closing to
clench like a fist, not powers-that-be who confuse and insist.

3 When broken is normal we need broken bread, the sign that all
brokenness is not the end. We feast on the promise a
new world will come; we praise God for Jesus, the new world begun.

Text: Richard Leach, 1992.
Music: Alfred V. Fedak, 1994.
Text and music © 1994, Selah Publishing Co., Inc. All rights reserved.

11 11 11 11
NEW WORLD

SOCIETY/SOCIAL CONCERNS

Empty Is the Manger 137

Unison

1 Empty is the manger; empty is the tomb; empty is the garden and the upper room. Once they gave Christ shelter, now he reigns above, and desires no dwelling save in hearts of love.

2 Empty is the pantry; empty is the purse; empty is the belly, breasts too dry to nurse. Millions wander, hungry; many die at birth, lacking deeds of mercy from this affluent earth.

3 Empty is the spirit; empty is the mind; empty of compassion, hearts no longer kind. People wander, aimless, swamped by useless toys, eyes enticed by baubles, ears entranced with noise.

4 Empty is the manger; empty is the tomb; empty is the garden and the upper room, for the Risen Savior reigns with God above, and his Holy Spirit dwells in hearts of love.

Text: Rae E. Whitney, 1989.
Music: Alec Wyton, 1993.
Text and music © 1994, Selah Publishing Co., Inc. All rights reserved.

65 65 D
HEARTS OF LOVE

SOCIETY/SOCIAL CONCERNS

138 Empty Is the Manger

1. Emp-ty is the man-ger; emp-ty is the tomb; emp-ty is the gar-den
2. Emp-ty is the pan-try; emp-ty is the purse; emp-ty is the bel-ly,
3. Emp-ty is the spir-it; emp-ty is the mind; emp-ty of com-pas-sion,
4. Emp-ty is the man-ger; emp-ty is the tomb; emp-ty is the gar-den

and the up-per room. Once they gave Christ shel-ter, now he reigns a-
breasts too dry to nurse. Mil-lions wan-der, hun-gry; man-y die at
hearts no long-er kind. Peo-ple wan-der, aim-less, swamped by use-less
and the up-per room, for the Ris-en Sav-ior reigns with God a-

Text: Rae E. Whitney, 1989.
Music: Alfred V. Fedak, 1994.
Text and music © 1994, Selah Publishing Co., Inc. All rights reserved.

65 65 D
EMPTY

bove   and de-sires no dwell - ing   save in hearts of love.
birth,   lack-ing deeds of mer - cy   from this af - fluent earth.
toys,   eyes en-ticed by bau - bles, ears en-tranced with noise.
bove,   and his Ho - ly Spir - it   dwells in hearts of love.

Alternate harmonization

SOCIETY/SOCIAL CONCERNS

139 God in His Love for Us

1. God in his love for us lent us this planet, gave it a purpose in time and in space; small as a spark from the fire of creation, cradle of life — and the home of our race.

2. Thanks be to God for its bounty and beauty, life that sustains us in body and mind; plenty for all if we learn how to share it, riches undreamed of to fathom and find.

3. Long have our human wars ruined its harvest; long has earth bowed to the terror of force; long have we wasted what others have need of, poisoned the fountain of life at its source.

4. Earth is the Lord's: it is ours to enjoy it, ours, as his stewards, to farm and defend. From its pollution, misuse, and damnation, good Lord, deliver us, — world without end.

Text: Fred Pratt Green, 1973. © 1973, The Hymn Society, TCU, Fort Worth, TX 76129. All rights reserved. Used by permission.
Music: David Ashley White, 1991. © 1991, Selah Publishing Co., Inc. All rights reserved.

11 10 11 10
JULIAN OF NORWICH

SOCIETY/SOCIAL CONCERNS

We Praise You, God, for Women   140

1 We praise you, God, for women who lived before their time,
  for prophets, priests, and abbesses, for poets with their rhyme.
  Great Hildegard of fiery tongue, Teresa, tireless, bold:
  such women lived with trust in you, and broke tradition's mold.

2 We praise you, God, for women who championed freedom's cause:
  Sojourner Truth and Rosa Parks, who challenged evil laws.
  They spoke the truth and held their ground, resisting what was wrong.
  They rested on your love and power; their courage makes us strong.

3 We praise you, God, for women who made your call their choice.
  The church denied, but they affirmed your Spirit's inward voice.
  They break the bread and bless the cup, though that was man's domain.
  Their priesthood opens worlds of grace to heal our grief and pain.

4 We praise you, God, for women who ventured paths unknown
  with faith that you had called them there and claimed them as your own.
  When we lose heart, then bring to mind the courage you bestow.
  The saints surround, a witness cloud to cheer us as we go.

Text: Ruth Duck, 1993, ©. Used by permission.
Music: Joy F. Patterson, 1993. © 1994 Selah Publishing Co., Inc. All rights reserved.

76 86 86 86
HILDEGARD OF BINGEN

OPENING OF WORSHIP
141 Now the Silence, Now the Peace

legato

Unison

1 Now the si-lence Now the peace Now the emp-ty hands up-
2 Then the glo-ry Then the rest Then the sab-bath peace un-

lift-ed Now the kneel-ing Now the plea Now the Fa-ther's
bro-ken Then the gar-den Then the throne Then the crys-tal

arms in wel-come Now the hear-ing Now the power
riv-er flow-ing Then the splen-dor Then the life

Text: Jaroslav J. Vajda, 1969, 1987. © 1969, 1987, Hope Publishing Co., Carol Stream, IL 60188.
All rights reserved. Used by permission.
Music: David Ashley White, 1992. © 1994, Selah Publishing Co., Inc. All rights reserved.

Irregular
SIMMS

Now the ves - sel brimmed for pour - ing / Now the Bo - dy
Then the new cre - a - tion sing - ing / Then the mar - riage

Now the Blood / Now the joy - ful cel - e - bra - tion / Now the wed - ding
Then the love / Then the feast of joy un - end - ing / Then the know - ing

Now the songs / Now the heart for - giv - en leap - ing / Now the Spir - it's
Then the light / Then the ul - ti - mate ad - ven - ture / Then the Spir - it's

vis - i - ta - tion / Now the Son's e - piph - a - ny / Now the Fa -
har - vest gath - ered / Then the Lamb in maj - es - ty / Then the Fa -

ther's bless - ing Now Now Now
ther's A - men Then Then Then

OPENING OF WORSHIP
142 Let Us Come Now to the Kingdom

1 Let us come now to the king-dom, where we're greet-ed by our Lord,
2 Let us come now to the king-dom, where all hun-gry souls are fed,

where our feet are washed in glo-ry and our en-er-gies re-stored,
where our drink is peace and glad-ness and God's righ-teous-ness our bread,

where the saints have come to join us from the west and from the east,
where each stran-ger is our neigh-bor and each neigh-bor next of kin,

where from north and south they've gath-ered to help cel-e-brate the feast!
where Christ waits for all God's chil-dren, so the ban-quet can be-gin!

Text: Rae E. Whitney, 1993. © 1994, Selah Publishing Co., Inc. All rights reserved.
Music: Donald Busarow, 1992. © 1992 MorningStar Music Publishers. All rights reserved. Used by permission.

87 87 D
ST. MATTHEW THE YOUNGER

OPENING OF WORSHIP

This Day God Gives Me   143

Unison

1. This day God gives me strength of high heaven, sun and moon shining, flame in my hearth, flashing of lightning, wind in its swiftness, deeps of the oceans, firmness of earth.
2. This day God sends me strength as my guardian, might to uphold me, wisdom as guide. Your eyes are watchful; your ears are listening; your lips are speaking, friend at my side.
3. God's way is my way; God's shield is round me; God's host defends me, saving from ill. Angels of heaven, drive from me always all that would harm me, stand by me still.
4. Rising, I thank you, mighty and strong One, King of creation, giver of rest, firmly confessing Threeness of Persons, Oneness of Godhead, Trinity blest.

Text: James Quinn, S.J., 1968, ©. Selah Publishing Co., Inc., U.S. agent.
Music: Russell Schulz-Widmar, 1994. © 1994 Selah Publishing Co., Inc. All rights reserved.

555 4 D
SANJEEV

OPENING OF WORSHIP

144 On Angels' and Archangels' Wings

1 On an-gels' and arch-an-gels' wings our hymns as-
2 Since God, the Lord of love-li-ness, knew mu-sic
3 Let cym-bals, strings, and trum-pets sound God's right-eous-
4 To hear our mu-sic God de-lights, and so, in

cend to touch God's throne; with all the com-pa-
would our souls up-lift, he gave the joy of
ness with one ac-cord; let or-gans swell, and
wor-ship joined as one with all the com-pan-

ny of heaven, we praise the Fa-ther, Spir-it, Son!
song to us; in love we now re-turn the gift!
peo-ple sing the lov-ing-kind-ness of our Lord!
y of heaven, we praise the Fa-ther, Spir-it, Son!

Text: Rae E. Whitney, 1985. © 1990, Selah Publishing Co., Inc. All rights reserved.
Music: English melody; harm. David N. Johnson, 1978 (from *Songs for the People of God*).
Harm. © 1994, Selah Publishing Co., Inc. All rights reserved.

LM
SUMMER COURT

CONFESSION AND FORGIVENESS
Vain Our Lives 145

1. Vain our lives, and small our strivings; all our gains are meaningless;
   groundless is our gift for boasting; until, we, our sins, confess!
   What we've twisted, we can't straighten; what we've lacked, we can't renew;
   what is worthless, we have worshiped; all our values are askew!

2. Vain our wisdom, small our science, when we trust our wits alone;
   vain our strength, and small our splendor, when we claim them as our own!
   With more wisdom comes more sorrow; with much knowledge comes much grief;
   with conceit, so comes affliction: God, alone, can grant relief!

3. Vain our pleasures, small our passions: all we long for, must we try?
   Charm is dimmed by acquisition: all we grasp for, must we buy?
   Of our trifles, soon we tire; at our tinkets, soon we yawn;
   vain, the goods which we acquire! Woe, the base we build upon!

4. God, forgive our selfish strivings; God, forget our foolish pride;
   God, uncover where we've wandered; in your mercy, may we hide!
   There, to face a new direction; there, to find a new resolve;
   there, to follow as you lead us; our vainglory, God, absolve!

Text: John A. Dalles, 1991.
Music: Alfred V. Fedak, 1993.
Text and music © 1994 Selah Publishing Co., Inc. All rights reserved.

87 87 D
KOHELET

CONFESSION AND FORGIVENESS

146 Forgive Me, Father, I Confess

1. Forgive me, Father, I confess dark dealings with unrighteousness; from my soiled heart, I pray, remove whatever keeps me from your love.
2. You formed me from the dust to be in likeness of the Trinity, but I have marred that image, so your truths in me no longer show.
3. When I, in Adam's sin, was caught, Christ, for my soul, salvation bought; baptized, I wore my Savior's sign; confirmed, I shared his bread and wine.
4. A member of your kingdom, then, until I strayed with godless men; I linked arms in their worldly dance and squandered my inheritance.

5 You waited long and patiently
because the choice now lay with me;
at last I to my senses came,
returning home in stumbling shame.

6 Dear Father, I repent to you;
restore me; my bruised heart renew;
and may the heavens in joy abound
because your child once more is found!

Text: Rae E. Whitney, 1981.
Music: David Ashley White, 1981.
Text and music © 1994, Selah Publishing Co., Inc. All rights reserved.

LM
SHERIDAN

DEDICATION AND OFFERING
Oh, I Believe That God   147

1 Oh, I believe that God created me and
ev-ery-thing, and dai-ly gives to me the life and strength I
need to sing such prais-es as I ought to bring to
God whose heart is love. This is most cer-tain-ly true.

2 I trust in Je-sus Christ, true God and true hu-
man-i-ty. He is my Lord and God for I was lost and
he saved me from sin and Sa-tan's ty-ran-ny so
I might be his own. This is most cer-tain-ly true.

3 For I am cer-tain I can-not be-lieve on
Christ as Lord by my own strength or thought. The Ho-ly Spir-it
through the Word has called, en-light-ened me, and stirred new
life, true faith in me. This is most cer-tain-ly true.

Text: *The Apostles' Creed*; para. Gracia Grindal, 1987.
Music: Mark Sedio, 1987.
Text and music © 1994 Selah Publishing Co., Inc. All rights reserved.

68 68 86 7
CREDO

WORD OF GOD

148 Word of God, Come Down on Earth

1. Word of God, come down on earth, living rain from heaven descending; touch our hearts and bring to birth faith and hope and love unending. Word almighty, we revere you; Word made flesh, we long to hear you.

2. Word eternal, throned on high, Word that brought to life creation, Word that came from heaven to die, crucified for our salvation, saving Word the world restoring, speak to us, your love outpouring.

3. Word that caused blind eyes to see, speak and heal our mortal blindness; deaf we are: our healer be; loose our tongues to tell your kindness. Be our Word in pity spoken; heal the world, by our sin broken.

4. Word that speaks God's tender love, one with God beyond all telling, Word that sends us from above, God the Spirit, with us dwelling, Word of truth, to all truth lead us; Word of life, with one Bread feed us.

Text: James Quinn, S.J., 1969, ©. Selah Publishing Co., Inc., U.S. agent.
Music: Johann R. Ahle, 1664.

78 78 88
LIEBSTER JESU

WORD OF GOD

The Word of God Was from the Start 149

1 The word of God was from the start. The word drove seas and
2 The word be-came a child of earth. The word ar-rived through
3 The word of God was hu-man-sized, the word by most un-
4 The word had first made flesh from sod, the word-made-flesh turned
5 The word shall be our life and light. The word shall be our

land a-part. The word made rocks and liv-ing things. The
hu-man birth. The word like us was blood and bone. The
rec-og-nized. The word by oth-ers was re-ceived. The
flesh toward God. The word is work-ing on flesh still. The
power and might. The word a-bove all wealth is priced. The

word raised up and brought down kings.
word knew life as we have known.
word gave life when they be-lieved.
word is spell-ing out God's will.
word by name is Je-sus Christ.

Text: Thomas H. Troeger, 1982. © 1982, Oxford University Press. All rights reserved. Used by permission.
Music: William P. Rowan, 1993. © 1993, Selah Publishing Co., Inc. All rights reserved.

LM
VERBUM DEI

WORD OF GOD

150 God Has Spoken by the Prophets

1 God has spoken by the prophets, spoken the unchanging Word;
  each from age to age proclaiming God the One, the righteous Lord!
  'Mid the world's despair and turmoil one firm anchor holding fast:

2 God has spoken by Christ Jesus, Christ, the everlasting Son,
  brightness of the Father's glory, with the Father ever one;
  spoken by the Word incarnate, God of God ere time was born;

3 God is speaking by the Spirit, speaking to our hearts again,
  in the age-long word declaring God's own message, now as then.
  Through the rise and fall of nations one sure faith is standing fast:

Text: George Wallace Briggs, alt. © 1953, renewed 1981, The Hymn Society, TCU, Forth Worth, TX 76129.
  All rights reserved. Used by permission.
Music: Sally Ann Morris, 1993. © 1994, Selah Publishing Co., Inc. All rights reserved.

87 87 D
FIRM ANCHOR

God e-ter-nal reigns for-ev-er, God the first and God the last.
Light of Light, to earth de-scend-ing, Christ, as God in hu-man form.
God a-bides, the Word un-chang-ing, God the first and God the last.

May This Water Keep Us Aware

BAPTISM
151

1 May this wa-ter keep us a-ware of the gift that we all share:
2 Wa-ter and the Spir-it give birth to a life of great-er worth,
3 Let us praise our Fath-er a-bove who, in his ex-trav-a-gant love,

graft-ed are we on Christ, the Vine, by the liv-ing wa-ter's sign.
for by them God's king-dom is ours, and we share his ho-ly powers.
sent his Spir-it and his Son, in the wa-ter made us one.

Text and music: Christopher Uehlein, 1972.
Text and music © 1994, Selah Publishing Co., Inc. All rights reserved.

87 87
CORDELL

LORD'S SUPPER

152 Come in Holy Awe and Truth

1. Come in holy awe and truth, brothers, sisters, to the altar;
   children in the bloom of youth, elders, come with steps that falter;
   all, of great or no renown, here, to God, we stand as one.

2. Those who live by cares oppressed, those who scamper through life gaily,
   those who know unruffled rest, those who weep in sorrow daily,
   friends and enemies, as one boldly come, approach the Throne.

3. By one cup and by one bread in one body, Lord, unite us;
   by the blood the Savior shed now with peace and joy delight us.
   Speak the good news once again. What more cause to sing, "Amen!"

4. By one washing, by one creed, each to all one Father binds us,
   one the hope on which we feed, one the grace that seeks and finds us;
   joined in love together so, to one Table let us go.

5. Here ourselves we consecrate
   to all truth, to love, to justice;
   by this action let us state
   what a holy people's trust is;
   show to all the Christ who lives,
   eat and drink the food he gives.

6. Tears of loneliness replace
   with new tears of happy laughter,
   children of adopting grace,
   see the home the world strives after:
   ours it is when we are one
   with the Father and the Son.

Text: Johann Friedrich Starke; Slovak tr. Jan Bohumil Ertel, 1745; tr. Jaroslav J. Vajda, 1971, 1975, ©. Used by permission.
Music: AnnaMae Meyer Bush, 1993. © 1994, Selah Publishing Co., Inc. All rights reserved.

78 78 77
AMANDA

LORD'S SUPPER
The Lord Is Here! 153

Unison

1. The Lord is here! His prom-ised word is ev-er-more the same, him-self to be where two or three are gath-ered in his Name.
2. The Lord is here! Where Christ is come his Spir-it, too, is there; with all who raise the song of praise or breathe the voice of prayer.
3. The Lord is here! He comes in peace with bless-ings from a-bove, by pledge and sign of bread and wine to fold us in his love.
4. The Lord is here! To ev-ery soul this gift of grace be given, to walk the way of Christ to-day, and share the life of heaven.

Text: Timothy Dudley-Smith, 1985. © 1988, Hope Publishing Co., Carol Stream, IL 60188. All rights reserved. Used by permission.
Music: Keith Landis, 1988; harm. Jeffrey Rickard, 1988. © 1994, Selah Publishing Co., Inc. All rights reserved.

CM
GRAHAM

LORD'S SUPPER

154 This Is the Hour

1 This is the hour of ban-quet and of song; this is the heaven-ly
2 Too soon we rise; we go our sev-eral ways; the feast, though not the
3 Feast af-ter feast thus comes and pass-es by, yet, pass-ing, points to

ta - ble spread for me; here let me feast, and feast-ing, still pro-
love, is past and gone, the Bread and Wine con-sumed: yet all our
the glad feast a - bove, giv-ing us fore-taste of the fes - tal

long the brief, bright hour of fel - low - ship with thee.
days thou still art here with us, our Shield and Sun.
joy, the Lamb's great mar - riage feast of bliss and love.

Text: Horatius Bonar.
Music: Joel Martinson, 1988. © 1994, Selah Publishing Co., Inc. All rights reserved.

10 10 10 10
BRUERN ABBEY

LORD'S SUPPER
And As They Ate 155

1 And as they ate Je-sus took bread, he blessed and broke it and
2 He took the cup; when he gave thanks, he gave it to them. They
3 "This is for you; it is the blood I shed for ma-ny. I
4 He said to them, "I will not drink a-gain of new wine un-
5 Lord, feed us food fi-ner than wheat: your bro-ken bo-dy; the

gave it to them. He said, "Take, eat, this is my bo-dy."
all drank of it. "This is my blood," Je-sus said, "Drink it."
free-ly give you my test-a-ment. It is the new wine."
til I taste it when I have come in-to God's king-dom."
rar-est vin-tage: your ho-ly blood giv-en to save us!

Text: Gracia Grindal, 1984.
Music: Mark Sedio, 1984.
Text and music © 1994, Selah Publishing Co., Inc. All rights reserved.

8 10 8
NEW WINE

LORD'S SUPPER

156 All Who Hunger, Gather Gladly

Unison

1 All who hunger, gather gladly; holy manna is our bread.
Come from wilderness and wand'ring. Here, in truth, we will be fed.

2 All who hunger, never strangers, seeker, be a welcome guest.
Come from restlessness and roaming. Here, in joy, we keep the feast.

3 All who hunger, sing together; Jesus Christ is living bread.
Come from loneliness and longing. Here, in peace, we have been led.

Harmony

You that yearn for days of fullness, all around us is our food.
We that once were lost and scattered in communion's love have stood.
Blest are those who from this table live their days in gratitude.

Unison

Taste and see the grace eternal. Taste and see that God is good.
Taste and see the grace eternal. Taste and see that God is good.
Taste and see the grace eternal. Taste and see that God is good.

Text: Sylvia Dunstan, 1990. © 1991, G.I.A. Publications. All rights reserved. Used by permission.
Music: David Ashley White, 1992. © 1994, Selah Publishing Co., Inc. All rights reserved.

87 87 D
DENSON

Optional interlude

[God is good.]

LORD'S SUPPER
Bread Is Blessed and Broken 157

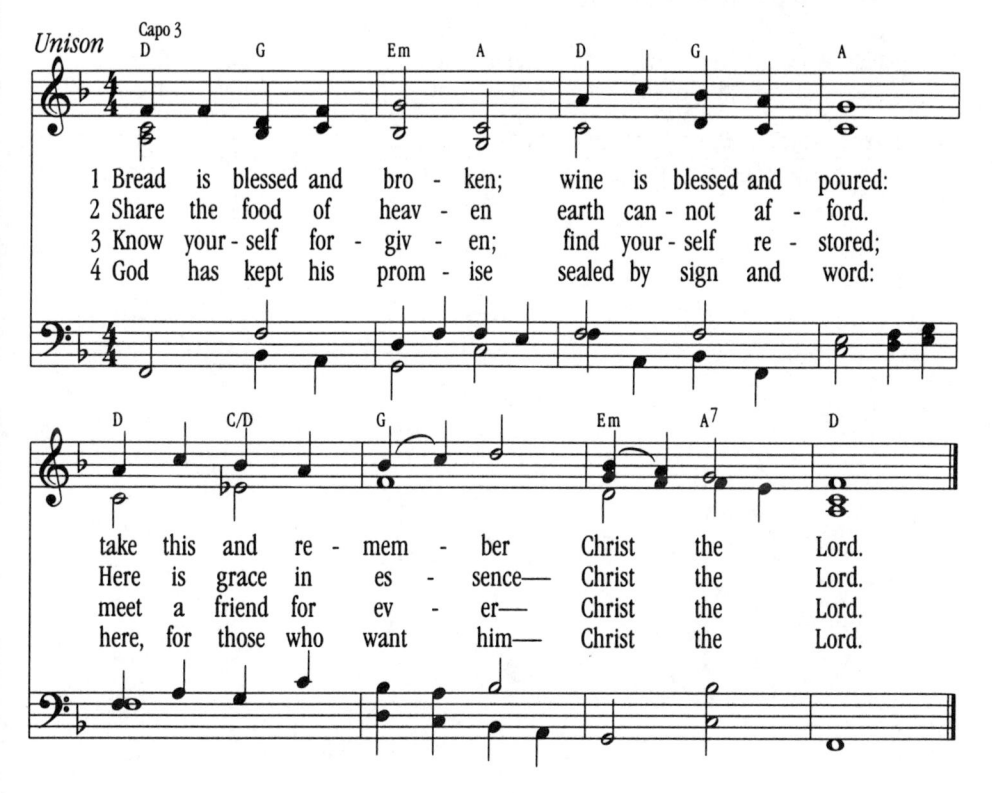

Unison

1 Bread is blessed and bro - ken; wine is blessed and poured:
2 Share the food of heav - en earth can - not af - ford.
3 Know your - self for - giv - en; find your - self re - stored;
4 God has kept his prom - ise sealed by sign and word:

take this and re - mem - ber Christ the Lord.
Here is grace in es - sence— Christ the Lord.
meet a friend for ev - er— Christ the Lord.
here, for those who want him— Christ the Lord.

Text: John Bell and Graham Maule. © 1989, The Iona Community. Used by permission of G.I.A. Publications.
Music: Keith Landis, 1993; harm. Alfred V. Fedak, 1993. © 1994, Selah Publishing Co., Inc. All rights reserved.

65 63
COLFAX

LORD'S SUPPER

158 Draw Nigh and Take

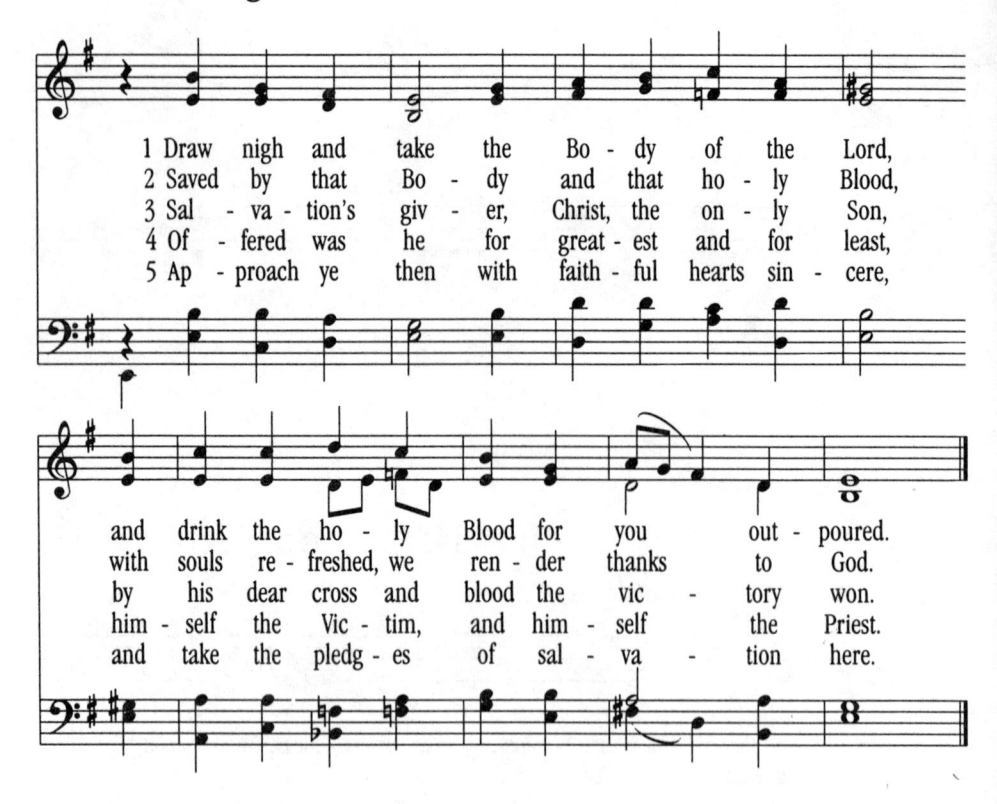

1 Draw nigh and take the Body of the Lord,
and drink the holy Blood for you out-poured.

2 Saved by that Body and that holy Blood,
with souls refreshed, we render thanks to God.

3 Salvation's giver, Christ, the only Son,
by his dear cross and blood the victory won.

4 Offered was he for greatest and for least,
himself the Victim, and himself the Priest.

5 Approach ye then with faithful hearts sincere,
and take the pledges of salvation here.

Text: *Bangor Antiphoner*, ca. 690; tr. J, Mason Neale, alt.
Music: David Ashley White, 1981. © 1994, Selah Publishing Co., Inc. All rights reserved.

10 10
PALMER CHURCH

LORD'S SUPPER

As a Child We Take This Bread 159

Descant

3 Like in Jesus' day, sharing bread the crowd to stay;

1 As a child we take this bread, by its substance we are fed.
2 Now we with a child-like grace, drink the cup in thirsty haste.
3 Like the child in Jesus' day, sharing bread the crowd to stay;

take the food these vessels bear; Christ is here to help us share.

When our hunger seeks the feast; Christ is here to feed the least.
Drawing from the fruited vine, Christ is here to give us wine.
take the food these vessels bear; Christ is here to help us share.

Text: Jim Miller, 1987.
Music: Thomas Pavlechko, 1993.
Text and music © 1994, Selah Publishing Co., Inc. All rights reserved.

77 77
HELLMERS

FUNERAL
160 Faithful Vigil Ended

1. Faithful vigil ended, watching, waiting cease;
Master, grant your servant *his discharge in peace.
All the Spirit promised, all the Father willed,
now these eyes behold it perfectly fulfilled.

2. This your great deliverance sets your people free;
Christ their light uplifted all the nations see.
Christ, your people's glory! watching, doubting cease;
grant to us your servants our discharge in peace.

*Note: *her* or *their* (with "servants") may be substituted for *his*.

Text: *Nunc Dimittis* (Luke 2:29-32); para. Timothy Dudley-Smith. © 1984, Hope Publishing Co., Carol Stream, IL 60188. All rights reserved. Used by permission.
Music: Leo Nestor, 1994. © 1994, Selah Publishing Co., Inc. All rights reserved.

65 65 D
WILLIAM

FUNERAL
We Are the Music Angels Sing 161

1 We are the music angels sing: short or long,
2 A child, brief sky-lark, soaring young, fell from sight,
3 The melody, though short it seems, deeper grows:
4 Discordant grief and aching night, love transposed,

each life a song, a treasured offering.
yet all that flight by Gabriel is sung.
heav'ns music flows, developing its themes.
will be composed in symphonies of light.

5 And every human pain and wrong
   shall be healed,
   for Christ revealed
   a new and better song.

6 We are the music angels sing:
   short or long,
   each life a song,
   a treasured offering.

Text: Brian Wren, 1988. © 1988, Hope Publishing Co., Carol Stream, IL 60188. All rights reserved. Used by permission.
Music: Alfred V. Fedak, 1990. © 1990, Selah Publishing Co., Inc. All rights reserved.

83 46
REITBERG

FUNERAL
162 Since You Have, Too, Encountered Grief

1. Since you have, too, encountered grief and felt the sting of tears, we come, dear Lord, in sure belief you understand our fears.
2. The one we love has left us now, and we all mourn his loss; yet still he's yours, for on his brow he bears baptism's cross.
3. He's often knelt where Christians kneel to take of holy bread; Lord, as we share your sacred meal, may we with strength be fed.
4. The emptiness of grief is ours, its sorrow and its pain; sharp thorns have sprung where once grew flowers and sunlight's lost in rain.
5. So comfort us as you know best, and guide us by your Word; as you have given our loved one rest, so give us courage, Lord.

Note: *She* and *her* may be substituted for *he* and *his*.

Text: Rae E. Whitney, 1981.
Music: Betty Carr Pulkingham, 1982.
Text and music © 1994, Selah Publishing Co., Inc. All rights reserved.

CM
HOLY SEED

O Gracious Light 163
EVENING

1. O gracious Light, Lord Jesus Christ, in you the Father's glory shone. Immortal, holy, blest is he, and blest are you, his holy Son.
2. Now sunset comes, but light shines forth; the lamps are lit to pierce the night. Praise Father, Son, and Spirit: God who dwells in the eternal light.
3. Worthy are you of endless praise, O Son of God, Life-giving Lord; wherefore you are through all the earth and in the highest heavens adored.

Text: *Phos Hilaron*, Greek, 3rd cent.; tr. F. Bland Tucker (1895-1984). © The Church Pension Fund. Used by permission.
Music: David Hurd, 1990. © 1994 Selah Publishing Co., Inc. All rights reserved.

LM
CYPRIAN

EVENING
164 O Light Whose Splendor

1. O Light whose splen-dor thrills and glad-dens with ra-diance bright-er than the sun, pure gleam of God's un-end-ing glo-ry, O Je-sus, blest A-noint-ed One;

2. as twi-light hov-ers near at sun-set, and lamps are lit, and chil-dren nod, in eve-ning hymns we lift our voic-es to Fa-ther, Spir-it, Son: one God.

3. In all life's bril-liant, time-less mo-ments, let faith-ful voic-es sing your praise, O Son of God, our Life-be-stow-er, whose glo-ry light-ens end-less days.

Text: *Phos hilaron*, Greek, 3rd. cent.; para. Carl P. Daw, Jr., 1989. © 1989, Hope Publishing Co., Carol Stream, IL 60188. All rights reserved. Used by permission.
Music: David Ashley White, 1986. © 1991, Selah Publishing Co., Inc. All rights reserved.

98 98
PHOS HILARON

Day Is Done

EVENING 165

1. Day is done, but Love un-fail-ing dwells ev-er here;
shadows fall, but hope, pre-vail-ing, calms ev-ery fear.
Lov-ing Fa-ther, none for-sak-ing, take our hearts, of Love's own mak-ing; watch our sleep-ing; guard our wak-ing; be al-ways near!

2. Dark de-scends, but Light un-end-ing shines through our night;
you are with us, ev-er lend-ing new strength to sight;
one in love, your truth con-fess-ing, one in hope of heav-en's bless-ing, may we see, in love's pos-sess-ing, Love's end-less light!

3. Eyes will close, but you, un-sleep-ing, watch by our side;
death may come: in Love's safe keep-ing still we a-bide.
God of love, all e-vil quell-ing, sin for-giv-ing, fear dis-pell-ing, stay with us, our hearts in-dwell-ing this e-ven-tide!

Text: James Quinn, S.J. 1969, ©. Selah Publishing Co., Inc., U.S. agent.
Music: Traditional Welsh melody.

84 84 88 84
AR HYD Y NOS

SPECIAL OCCASIONS

166 Grey Ashes Fall

Unison

1. Grey ashes fall where flames have burned, and silence
speaks where noise was dumb; the present from the past has
turned to see the future come.

2. The past a heavy burden weighs, and present
debts hang still unpaid; uncertain are the future
days to flourish or to fade.

3. The future comes; stirred by this life new fire within
the dust glows red, till, overcoming death in
strife, bright flames rise from the dead.

Text: Rae E. Whitney, 1948.
Music: Austin C. Lovelace, 1989.
Text and music © 1994, Selah Publishing Co., Inc. All rights reserved.

88 86
EMBERS

SPECIAL OCCASIONS

Now Greet the Swiftly Changing Year 167

1 Now greet the swift-ly chang-ing year with joy and pen-i-tence sin-cere; re-joice, re-joice, with thanks em-brace an-oth-er year of grace.
2 This Je-sus came to wage sin's war; the Name of names for us he bore; re-joice, re-joice, with thanks em-brace an-oth-er year of grace.
3 His love a-bun-dant far ex-ceeds the vol-ume of a whole year's needs; re-joice, re-joice, with thanks em-brace an-oth-er year of grace.
4 With such a Lord to lead our way in want and in pros-per-i-ty, what need we fear in earth or space in this new year of grace?
5 "All glo-ry be to God on high and peace on earth," the an-gels cry; re-joice, re-joice, with thanks em-brace an-oth-er year of grace.

Text: Slovak, 17th cent.; tr. Jaroslav J. Vajda, 1968, alt. © 1969, Concordia Publishing House. All rights reserved.
Used by permission.
Music: Alfred V. Fedak, 1984. © 1990, Selah Publishing Co., Inc. All rights reserved.

88 86
SIXTH NIGHT

SPECIAL OCCASIONS

168 Upstairs? Downstairs?

1 Up-stairs? Down-stairs? God is there! God is here and ev-ery-where.
  In the church and in the street, God is there for all to meet.
2 Met in cir-cles, large and small, we keep list-ening to God's call,
  keen in love and faith to grow, more of Christ-for-life to know.
3 As you leave us, so we pray: "Peace be with you on your way."
  "Peace with you, who stay be-hind; God be in your heart and mind."

Text: Fred Kaan, 1987. © 1989, Hope Publishing Co., Carol Stream, IL 60188. All rights reserved. Used by permission.
Music: Alfred V. Fedak, 1990. © 1990, Selah Publishing Co., Inc. All rights reserved.

77 77
UPSTAIRS, DOWNSTAIRS

CLOSE OF WORSHIP

Forth in the Peace of Christ We Go 169

1. Forth in the peace of Christ we go; Christ to the
lips, Christ in our hearts, the world's true King.

2. Priests of the world, Christ sends us forth the world of
time to con-se-crate, the world of sin by grace to
heal, Christ's world in Christ to re - cre - ate.

3. Christ's are our lips, his word we speak; proph-ets are
we whose deeds pro-claim Christ's truth in love that we may
be Christ in the world, to spread Christ's name.

4. We are the church; Christ bids us show that in his
church all na-tions find their hearth and home, where Christ restores true peace, true love, to hu-man-kind.

Text: James Quinn, S.J., 1969, ©. Selah Publishing Co., Inc., U.S. agent.
Music: Georg Joseph, 1657, adapt.

LM
ANGELUS

CLOSE OF WORSHIP

170 Lord, Bid Your Servant Go in Peace

1. Lord, bid your servant go in peace; your word is now fulfilled.
   These eyes have seen salvation's dawn, this child so long foretold.
2. This is the Savior of the world, the Gentiles' promised light,
   God's glory dwelling in our midst, the joy of Israel.

Text: *Song of Simeon* (Luke 2:29-32); para. James Quinn, S.J., 1969, ©. Selah Publishing Co., Inc., U.S. agent.
Music: American folk tune; harm. Russell Schulz-Widmar, 1983 (from *Songs for the People of God*).
Harm. © 1994, Selah Publishing Co., Inc. All rights reserved.

CM
LAND OF REST

CLOSE OF WORSHIP
Now Have You Set Your Servant Free 171

(Cantor) *(All)*

Now have you set your servant free, O Lord, to go in peace according to your word. For I have seen your promised victory in One prepared for all the world to see: a Light for nations who in darkness dwell, the glory of your people Is-ra-el.

Text: *Song of Simeon* (Luke 2:29-32); para. Carl P. Daw, Jr., 1990. © 1990, Hope Publishing Co., Carol Stream, IL 60188. All rights reserved. Used by permission.
Music: David Ashley White, 1986. © 1991 Selah Publishing Co., Inc. All rights reserved.

10 10 10 10 10 10
NUNC DIMITTIS

Copyright Holders

We are grateful to the individuals and publishers who have granted us permission to print their copyrighted material in *New Songs of Rejoicing*. If you wish to reproduce any work contained in this book, contact the copyright holder for permission. Current addresses of individuals holding copyrights may be requested from Selah Publishing Co., Inc.

Selah Publishing Co., Inc. and many of these publishers participate in licensing agencies such as C.C.L.I. and LicenSing. Permission to use most of the hymns in *New Songs of Rejoicing* may be requested from such agencies.

Augsburg Fortress Publishers
426 S. Fifth Ave./Box 1209
Minneapolis, MN 55440
(612) 330-3300

The Church Hymnal Corporation
800 Second Ave.
New York, NY 10017
(800) 223-6602

Concordia Publishing House
3558 S. Jefferson Ave.
St. Louis, MO 63118
(314) 664-7000

G.I.A. Publications
7404 S. Mason Ave.
Chicago, IL 60638
(312) 496-3800

Hope Publishing Co.
380 S. Main Pl.
Carol Stream, IL 60188
(800) 323-1049

The Hymn Society
in the United States and Canada
c/o Hope Publishing Co.

MorningStar Music Publishers
2117 59th St.
St. Louis, MO 63110
(314) 647-2117

Oxford University Press
200 Madison Ave.
New York, NY 10016
(212) 679-7300

Selah Publishing Co., Inc.
P.O. Box 3037
Kingston, NY 12401
(800) 852-6172

One-time license for Selah copyrights

We at Selah Publishing Co. understand the nature of church work, and to facilitate the use of hymns for which Selah holds the copyright, the license below may be used whenever you wish to use a hymn in a congregational worship service. A one-time fee of $10 (until December 31, 1995) is required for each hymn used, but it is our hope that this arrangement will allow these hymns to be used more often and with less paperwork for church workers. Please note the following conditions and restrictions. Violation of any of these conditions will be considered copyright infringement. Contact Selah Publishing Co. for information on a one-year license or for other use.

This license is only for congregational use.
This license is only for hymns where **Selah holds the copyright for both text and music**
    (or if the accompanying text or music are in the public domain).
The hymns may not be altered in any way.
The credits and copyright notice must appear on the printed page and the text "Used by permission."
The fee must be submitted with a copy of the form below completely filled in.
After December 31, 1995, contact Selah Publishing Co., Inc. for a revised form and fee schedule.

```
Church name _____

Contact person _____

Address _____

_____

Phone no. _____

Title of hymn/author _____

Tune name/composer _____

Date used _____   Number of copies made _____

        Remit with $10 fee to Selah Publishing Co., Inc. P.O. Box 3037, Kingston, NY 12401 • Expires 12/31/95
```

Anthem Settings of Hymns

As Panting Deer
Carl P. Daw, Jr./David Ashley White
(Selah—410-842)

Hope Is the Harrowing
Richard Leach/David Ashley White
(Selah—420-622)

Isaiah the Prophet
Joy F. Patterson/Austin C. Lovelace
(Selah—405-111)

King of Glory, King of Peace
Herbert/David Charles Walker, arr. Brewer
(Selah—418-609)

Lord, Make Us Servants of Your Peace
James Quinn/K. Lee Scott
(Selah—425-822)

Not for Tongues of Heaven's Angels
Timothy Dudley-Smith/Roy Hopp
(Selah—425-812)

Now Greet the Swiftly Changing Year
Jaroslav J. Vajda/Alfred V. Fedak
(Concordia—98-2691)

Now Thank We All Our God–Hal H. Hopson
(Selah—410-676)

O Jesus I Have Promised–David Ashley White
(MorningStar Music Publishers—50-9055)

They Cast Their Nets in Galilee
(The Fisherfolk)-Percy/Betty Pulkingham
(Selah—420-866)

We Have Come at Christ's Own Bidding
(This Glimpse of Glory)
Carl P. Daw, Jr./David Ashley White
(Augsburg—11-10201)

When God's Time Had Ripened
Carl P. Daw, Jr./Alfred V. Fedak
(Selah—405-214)

Without the Fire
Rae E. Whitney/David Ashley White
(Selah—410-275)

Woman in the Night
Brian Wren/William P. Rowan
(Selah—425-815)

Songs Appropriate for Children

As a Child We Take This Bread 159
And Jesus Said 69
Bread Is Blessed and Broken 157
Christ Be Beside Me 114
Come to Me, O Weary Traveler 66
Day Is Done 165
Empty Is the Manger 137, 138
Father in Heaven 65
Give Thanks to the Lord 58
Give with Simplicity 113
Hope Is a Star 12
Hosanna, Hosanna! 29
How Far Is It to Bethlehem? 15
If I Could Visit Bethlehem 14
Isaiah the Prophet 2
Lord, Glorify Yourself Today 118
Lord, Make Me an Alleluia 116, 117
Lord, Make Us Servants 100, 101
Music and Incense 92
O Child of Promise, Come! 1
Oh, I Believe That God 147
O Jesus, I Have Promised 125
O Joseph 18
Old Abraham Fell Down 78
Ol' Noah Got Mad 60
Onward, You Saints 89
Our Father in Heaven 64
Since You Are Shepherd 44
Terra Sancta, Holy Land 99
The Empty-Handed Fishermen 72
The Lord My Pasture Shall Prepare 45
There a Friend Is Weeping 119
They Have No Wine 71
Town of David 13
Upstairs? Downstairs? 168
What Are These Wounds 34
What Can I Ask in Your Name 107
When Jesus Entered Jericho 70
When the Lord Restored Our Fortunes 57
Without the Fire 127
Young Mary Lived in Nazareth 6

Scriptural Index

Genesis
1
    The Word of God Was from the Start 149
1:3
    Before the Earth Was Tossed in Space 76
1:26-27
    Forgive Me, Father, I Confess 146
    O God Who Made Us in Your Likeness 90
1:27-31
    God in His Love for Us 139
7-9
    Ol' Noah Got Mad 60
17:17
    Old Abraham Fell Down 78
18:1-15
    Old Abraham Fell Down 78
21:1-7
    Old Abraham Fell Down 78
32:24-32
    O God, on Whom We Lost Our Hold 132

Exodus
3:1-6
    Bush by the Fire Illumed 98
13:21
    Guided by God's Holy Grace 129
19:3
    Before the Earth Was Tossed in Space 76
33:11
    Before the Earth Was Tossed in Space 76

I Kings
19:12-13
    Before the Earth Was Tossed in Space 76

Job
28
    God in His Love for Us 139

Psalms
1:2-3
    By Your Streams of Living Waters 61
8:4
    Sing, My Soul, His Wondrous Love 85
19:7-14
    Your Law, O Lord, Is Perfect 43
23
    Since You Are Shepherd 44
    The Lord My Pasture Shall Prepare 45
24:1
    God in His Love for Us 139
    We Are Not Our Own 80
24:7-10
    Who Is This King of Glory? 46
32
    How Blessed Are Those 47
34:8
    All Who Hunger, Gather Gladly 156
42:1-5
    As Panting Deer 48
56
    In God I Trust 49
84
    Onward, You Saints 89
85
    Our God Forgives Us 50
90
    Now Greet the Swiftly Changing Year 167
95:1-7
    Come, Let Us Raise a Joyful Sound 51
    To God with Gladness Sing 52
110:1-4
    You Are a Priest Forever 55
119:164
    King of Glory, King of Peace 83
122:1
    Now the Silence, Now the Peace 141
126
    When the Lord Restored Our Fortunes 57
130
    In Deep Despair I Cry to You 59
136
    Give Thanks to the Lord 58

Isaiah
1:4-9
    God in His Love for Us 139
6:3
    We Praise You, O God 82
6:8
    There a Friend Is Weeping 119
7:14
    O Child of Promise, Come! 1
9:6
    O Child of Promise, Come! 1
11:1
    A Babe Is Born 11
    When God's Time Had Ripened 8
11:1-9
    Isaiah the Prophet 2
12:2-6
    Surely It Is God Who Saves Me 121, 122
42:1
    O Child of Promise, Come! 1
53:3-4
    O Child of Promise, Come! 1
55:1-6
    Come, Satisfy Your Thirst 62
55:12-13
    Isaiah the Prophet 2

Habakkuk
2:20
    Now the Silence, Now the Peace 141

SCRIPTURAL INDEX

Matthew
1:18-22
    O Joseph 18
    Young Mary Lived in Nazareth 6
2:1-12
    Before the Earth Was Tossed in Space 76
    Sing of God Made Manifest 17
    That King before Whose Majesty 16
2:14
    Who Better Than Mary 20
3:13-17
    Sing of God Made Manifest 17
3:16
    Dove to Flesh 42
4:18-22
    They Cast Their Nets in Galilee 63
5:11-12
    Give with Simplicity 113
6:9-13
    Father in Heaven 65
    Our Father in Heaven 64
6:19-20
    Sorrow and Gladness 135
8:11
    Let Us Come Now to the Kingdom 142
8:23-27
    Light of the Minds That Know Him 109
11:28-30
    Come to Me, O Weary Traveler 66
14:13-21
    They Have No Wine 71
17:1-8
    Before the Earth Was Tossed in Space 76
    Sing of God Made Manifest 17
    We Have Come at Christ's Own Bidding 23
18:20
    The Lord Is Here! 153
21:1-11
    Hosanna, Hosanna! 29
26:6-14
    Myrrh-Bearing Mary 67, 68
27:45-56
    How Shallow Former Shadows Seem 33
27:55-56
    Who Better Than Mary 20
    Woman in the Night 21, 22
27:56
    Myrrh-Bearing Mary 67, 68
28:1
    Woman in the Night 21, 22
28:5-7
    The Tomb Is Empty 35

Mark
1:9-11
    Sing of God Made Manifest 17
1:10
    Dove to Flesh 42
1:12-13
    Where Was the Greater Struggle? 27
4:35-41
    Light of the Minds That Know Him 109
6:3
    O Carpenter 24
6:30-44
    They Have No Wine 71
9:2-8
    Before the Earth Was Tossed in Space 76
    Sing of God Made Manifest 17
    We Have Come at Christ's Own Bidding 23
11:1-10
    Hosanna, Hosanna! 29
15:33-41
    How Shallow Former Shadows Seem 33
15:40
    Who Better Than Mary 20
15:40-41
    Woman in the Night 21, 22
16:1-8
    Woman in the Night 21, 22
16:9
    Myrrh-Bearing Mary 67, 68

Luke

1:26-38
    Told of God's Favor 3
1:26-45
    Young Mary Lived in Nazareth 6
1:38
    Who Better Than Mary 20
1:46-55
    My Soul Proclaims with Wonder 4
1:67-79
    Blessed Be the God of Israel 5
2:1-7
    Who Better Than Mary 20
    Woman in the Night 21, 22
    Young Mary Lived in Nazareth 6
2:1-20
    A Babe Is Born 11
2:14
    Now Greet the Swiftly Changing Year 167
2:28-36
    Sing of God Made Manifest 17
    We Have Come at Christ's Own Bidding 23
2:29-32
    Faithful Vigil Ended 160
    Lord, Bid Your Servant Go in Peace 170
    Now Have You Set Your Servant Free 171
2:41-52
    O Joseph 18
3:21-22
    Sing of God Made Manifest 17
3:22
    Dove to Flesh 42
4:18-19
    O Child of Promise, Come! 1
7:36-39
    Woman in the Night 21, 22
8:22-25
    Light of the Minds That Know Him 109
8:43-48
    Woman in the Night 21, 22
9:10-17
    They Have No Wine 71
9:28-36
    Before the Earth Was Tossed in Space 76
    Sing of God Made Manifest 17
    We Have Come at Christ's Own Bidding 23
11:2-4
    Father in Heaven 65
    Our Father in Heaven 64
15
    And Jesus Said 69
15:11-24
    Forgive Me, Father, I Confess 146
19:1-10
    When Jesus Entered Jericho 70
22:14-20
    And As They Ate 155
23:44-49
    How Shallow Former Shadows Seem 33

24:1-12
    Woman in the Night 21, 22
24:13-35
    Light of the Minds That Know Him 109
24:39
    What Are These Wounds 34

John

1:1-3
    Word of God, Come Down on Earth 148
1:1-5
    How Shallow Former Shadows Seem 33
1:1-14
    The Word of God Was from the Start 149
1:4
    Where You Are, There Is Life 79
1:14
    With the Body That Was Broken 31
2:1-11
    Sing of God Made Manifest 17
    They Have No Wine 71
4:7-26
    Woman in the Night 21, 22
6:35-38
    When God's Time Had Ripened 8
11:35
    Since You Have, Too, Encountered Grief 162
11:43
    Where You Are, There Is Life 79
11:43-44
    When Lazarus Lay within the Tomb 37
14:2
    The House of Faith 108
14:6
    Come My Way, My Truth, My Life 126
    O God of Spring and Summer Days 106
14:6, 23, 27
    Where You Are, There Is Life 79
15:1-5
    May This Water Keep Us Aware 151
17:20-21
    We Who Preach a Church United 97
19:25-26
    Who Better Than Mary 20
20:10-18
    Myrrh-Bearing Mary 67, 68
20:25-27
    What Are These Wounds 34
21:1-14
    The Empty-Handed Fisherman 72

Acts
1:9-11
    Praise Him As He Mounts the Skies 38
1:14
    Who Better Than Mary 20
2:1-4
    Come, Holy Spirit, Revive Your Church 40
    Dove to Flesh 42
    When Christians Shared Agape Meals 96
2:42-47
    When Christians Shared Agape Meals 96
14:14-17
    God in His Love for Us 139

Romans
8:34
    Praise Him As He Mounts the Skies 38
12:14
    Give with Simplicity 113
15:7
    Help Us Accept Each Other 110
15:20-26, 55-57
    Make Songs of Joy 36

I Corinthians
2:9
    Now the Silence, Now the Peace 141
10:16-17
    Come in Holy Awe and Truth 152
10:26
    God in His Love for Us 139
13:1-7
    Not for Tongues of Heaven's Angels 73
15:20-26, 55-57
    Make Songs of Joy 36

II Corinthians
4:13-18
    Now the Silence, Now the Peace 141
5:18-6:1
    We Are Ambassadors for Christ 74

Galatians
4:1
    When God's Time Had Ripened 8
5:22
    O God in Whom All Life Begins 105

Ephesians
3:16-19
    By Your Streams of Living Water 61
4:4-6
    Come in Holy Awe and Truth 152

Philippians
4:4-7
    Rejoice in Christ Jesus 75

Hebrews
1:1-2
    God Has Spoken by the Prophets 150
4:12
    God's Judgment Comes Like Fire 133
13:8
    O God of Spring and Summer Days 106

I Peter
2:21-23
    Give with Simplicity 113

I John
2:1
    Praise Him As He Mounts the Skies 38
4:7-12
    Love Is of God 124

Revelation
1:18
    Rejoice, the Lord Is King! 134
15:3-4
    We Marvel at Your Mighty Deeds 81
19:9
    This Is the Hour 154
19:16
    Praise Him As He Mounts the Skies 38

Topical Index

Adoration: see Praise and Adoration

Advent
Blessed Be the God of Israel 5
Mary, Woman of the Promise 7
My Soul Proclaims with Wonder 4
O Child of Promise, Come! 1
Told of God's Favor 3
Young Mary Lived in Nazareth 6

Afflictions
Come to Me, O Weary Traveler 66
God in His Love for Us 139
In Deep Despair I Cry to You 59
In God I Trust 49
O God of Spring and Summer Days 106
O God, on Whom We Lost Our Hold 132
O Jesus, I Have Promised 125
The Lord My Pasture Shall Prepare 45
There a Friend Is Weeping 119
They Cast Their Nets in Galilee 63
When Broken Is Normal 136

Aging: see Brevity and Frailty of Life

Alleluias
(see also Praise and Adoration)
Lord, Make Me an Alleluia 116, 117
Make Songs of Joy 36
Praise Him As He Mounts the Skies 38
Praise the Living God Who Sings 88

Angels
On Angels' and Archangels' Wings 144

Annunciation
My Soul Proclaims with Wonder 4
Told of God's Favor 3
Young Mary Lived in Nazareth 6

Ascension & Reign of Christ
(see also King, God/Christ as)
Before the Earth Was Tossed in Space 76
Christ the King, Enthroned in Splendor 39
Empty Is the Manger 137, 138
Glory to Christ on High! 87
O Lord, Eternal Light of God 19
Praise Him As He Mounts the Skies 38
Rejoice, the Lord Is King! 134
Sing, My Soul, His Wondrous Love 85
Who Is This King of Glory? 46

Assurance
(see also Faithfulness of God, Refuge, Trust in God)
My Soul Proclaims with Wonder 4
O God of Spring and Summer Days 106
Rejoice in Christ Jesus 75
Since You Are Shepherd 44
Surely It Is God Who Saves Me 121, 122

Atonement
Forgive Me, Father, I Confess 146
Rejoice in Christ Jesus 75

Baptism
Bush by the Fire Illumed 98
May This Water Keep Us Aware 151

Benediction: see Close of Worship
Benevolence: see Commitment & Dedication, Poverty, Stewardship
Bible: see Word of God

Biblical Names and Places
Abraham
Blessed Be the God of Israel 5
Old Abraham Fell Down 78
Bethlehem
How Far Is It to Bethlehem? 15
Terra Sancta, Holy Land 99
The Babe in Beth'lem's Manger Laid 10
Town of David 13
Cana
Sing of God Made Manifest 17
Elijah
Before the Earth Was Tossed in Space 76
Isaiah
Isaiah the Prophet 2
Isaac
Old Abraham Fell Down 78
John
They Cast Their Nets in Galilee 63
John the Baptist
Sing of God Made Manifest 17
Joseph
O Joseph 18
Lazarus
When Lazarus Lay within the Tomb 37
Where You Are, There Is Life 79
Mary Magdalene
Myrrh-Bearing Mary 67, 68
Woman in the Night 21, 22
Mary, Mother of Jesus
If I Could Visit Bethlehem 14
Mary, Woman of the Promise 7
My Soul Proclaims with Wonder 4
That King before Whose Majesty 16
Told of God's Favor 3
Who Better Than Mary 20
Woman in the Night 21, 22
Young Mary Lived in Nazareth 6

202

Biblical Names and Places *(continued)*
Moses
Before the Earth Was Tossed in Space 76
Bush by the Fire Illumed 98
Wondrous God, More Named Than Known 128
Nazareth
Terra Sancta, Holy Land 99
Noah
Ol' Noah Got Mad 60
Peter
They Cast Their Nets in Galilee 63
Sarah
Old Abraham Fell Down 78
Simeon
Lord, Bid Your Servant Go in Peace 170
Now Have You Set Your Servant Free 171
Wise Men
Before the Earth Was Tossed in Space 76
Sing of God Made Manifest 17
That King before Whose Majesty 16
Zacchaeus
And Jesus Said 69
When Jesus Entered Jericho 70
Zachariah
Blessed Be the God of Israel 5

Birth of Christ: see Christmas

Blood of Christ
All Who Hunger, Gather Gladly 156
And As They Ate 155
Bread Is Blessed and Broken 157
Come in Holy Awe and Truth 152
Draw Nigh and Take 158
This Is the Hour 154
What Are These Wounds 34
Who Better Than Mary 20
With the Body That Was Broken 31

Body of Christ
All Who Hunger, Gather Gladly 156
And As They Ate 155
Bread Is Blessed and Broken 157
Come in Holy Awe and Truth 152
Draw Nigh and Take 158
This Is the Hour 154
What Are These Wounds 34
Who Better Than Mary 20
With the Body That Was Broken 31

Bread of Life
All Who Hunger, Gather Gladly 156
Light of the Minds That Know Him 109
When God's Time Had Ripened 8
Without the Fire 127

Brevity and Frailty of Life
O God of Spring and Summer Days 106

Burdens: see Afflictions

Children
How Far Is It to Bethlehem? 15
Lord, Make Me an Alleluia 116, 117
Ol' Noah Got Mad 60
When Jesus Entered Jericho 70

Christian Life
(see also Pilgrimage and Conflict)
Bush by the Fire Illumed 98
Christ Be Beside Me 114
Come to Me, O Weary Traveler 66
Day by Day 123
Forgive Me, Father, I Confess 146
Grant Us Wisdom to Perceive You 103
Heirs Together of God's Grace 120
Help Us Accept Each Other 110
Into Our Loneliness 91
Light of the Minds That Know Him 109
Lord, Glorify Yourself Today 118
Lord, Make Us Saints 102
Lord, Make Us Servants 100, 101
Love Is of God 124
O God in Whom All Life Begins 105
O God of Spring and Summer Days 106
O Jesus, I Have Promised 125
Onward, You Saints 89
Sorrow and Gladness 135
Teach Us, Good Lord, to Serve 104
The House of Faith 108
The Lord My Pasture Shall Prepare 45
There a Friend Is Weeping 119
They Cast Their Nets in Galilee 63
This Day God Gives Me 143
We Are Not Our Own 80
Were the World to End Tomorrow 115
Where You Are, There Is Life 79
With Sounds of Gentle Stillness 112

Christmas
A Babe Is Born 11
Away with Our Fears 9
Hope Is a Star 12
How Far Is It to Bethlehem? 15
If I Could Visit Bethlehem 14
O Lord, Eternal Light of God 19
Sing of God Made Manifest 17
That King before Whose Majesty 16
The Babe in Beth'lem's Manger Laid 10
Town of David 13
When God's Time Had Ripened 8
Young Mary Lived in Nazareth 6

TOPICAL INDEX

Church
All Who Hunger, Gather Gladly 156
Bush by the Fire Illumed 98
Come Holy Spirit, Revive Your Church 40
Come in Holy Awe and Truth 152
Heirs Together of God's Grace 120
Let Us Come Now to the Kingdom 142
Lord, Make Us Saints 102
O God in Whom All Life Begins 105
Of Women and of Women's Hopes 130
Onward, You Saints 89
Taking Bread to Bless and Break 95
Terra Sancta, Holy Land 99
The Lord Is Here! 153
We Are Ambassadors for Christ 74
We Are Not Our Own 80
We Praise You God, for Women 140
We Who Preach a Church United 97
When Christians Shared Agape Meals 96

City: see Society/Social Concerns

Close of Worship
Day Is Done 165
Forth in the Peace of Christ We Go 169
Lord, Bid Your Servant Go in Peace 170
Now Have You Set Your Servant Free 171
O Gracious Light 163
O Light Whose Splendor 164

Comfort and Encouragement
(see also Doubt)
As Panting Deer 48
Bush by the Fire Illumed 98
Christ Be Beside Me 114
Come to Me, O Weary Traveler 66
God of Unknown, Distant Worlds 77
God Whose Love We Cannot Measure 84
In God I Trust 49
Music and Incense 92
Now the Silence, Now the Peace 141
O God in Whom All Life Begins 105
Our God Forgives Us 50
Rejoice in Christ Jesus 75
Since You Are Shepherd 44
Sorrow and Gladness 135
The House of Faith 108
The Lord My Pasture Shall Prepare 45
There a Friend Is Weeping 119
When the Lord Restored Our Fortunes 57

Commitment and Dedication
(see also Offering, Profession of Faith)
If I Could Visit Bethlehem 14
Oh, I Believe That God 147

Communion: see Lord's Supper

Communion of the Saints
Heirs Together of God's Grace 120
Let Us Come Now to the Kingdom 142
Music and Incense 92
O God in Whom All Life Begins 105
Onward, You Saints 89
We Praise You God, for Women 140
We Who Preach a Church United 97

Confession of Sin
(see also Forgiveness)
How Blessed Are Those 47
Sovereign Maker of All Things 28
Sunday's Palms Are Wednesday's Ashes 25, 26
Vain Our Lives 145

Conflict: see Pilgrimage & Conflict

Covenant
(see also Promises)
Blessed Be the God of Israel 5
Heirs Together of God's Grace 120
Now Thank We All Our God 86
Onward, You Saints 89
We Are Not Our Own 80

Creation
Before the Earth Was Tossed in Space 76
Come, Let Us Raise a Joyful Sound 51
God in His Love for Us 139
God of Grace and God of Laughter 131
God of Unknown, Distant Worlds 77
Isaiah the Prophet 2
Now Thank We All Our God 86
O God Who Made Us in Your Likeness 90
O Lord, Eternal Light of God 19
Praise the Living God Who Sings 88
Send Forth Your Spirit, O Lord 54
We Are Not Our Own 80
We Marvel at Your Mighty Deeds 81
We Praise You, O God 82
Where You Are, There Is Life 79

Creeds
Oh, I Believe That God 147
We Praise You, O God 82

Cross of Christ
(see also Suffering of Christ, Lent, Holy Week)
Before the Earth Was Tossed in Space 76
How Shallow Former Shadows Seem 33
Three Tall Trees Grew on a Windy Hill 32
What Are These Wounds 34
With the Body That Was Broken 31

Death of Christ: see Cross of Christ, Suffering of Christ
Death of Christians: see Funerals
Dedication: see Commitment & Dedication

Deliverance
(see also Redemption, Salvation)
Forgive Me, Father, I Confess 146
In God I Trust 49
Into Our Loneliness 91
O Carpenter 24
O Child of Promise, Come! 1
Our God Forgives Us 50
Sovereign Maker of All Things 28
Sunday's Palms Are Wednesday's Ashes 25, 26
Surely It Is God Who Saves 121, 122
When the Lord Restored 57

Death
Faithful Vigil Ended 160
Make Songs of Joy 36
Since You Have, Too, Encountered Grief ... 162
We Are the Music Angels Sing 161

Discipleship: see Walk with God

Doubt
(see also Comfort & Encouragement)
As Panting Deer 48
Come to Me, O Weary Traveler 66
God Whose Love We Cannot Measure 84
Music and Incense 92
Rejoice in Christ Jesus 75
Sorrow and Gladness 135
When the Lord Restored Our Fortunes 57

Easter
Make Songs of Joy 36
Myrrh-Bearing Mary 67, 68
On This Day the Lord Has Acted 56
The Tomb Is Empty! 35
When Lazarus Lay within the Tomb 37

Ecology: see Society/Social Concerns, Stewardship
Encouragement: see Comfort & Encouragement

Enemies and Persecution
(see also Laments)
In God I Trust 49

Epiphany and Ministry of Christ
O Carpenter 24
Sing of God Made Manifest 17
That King before Whose Majesty 16
Three Tall Trees Grew on a Windy Hill 32
We Have Come at Christ's Own Bidding 23
Who Better Than Mary 20
Woman in the Night 21, 22

Eternal Life
Come, Satisfy Your Thirst 62
Music and Incense 92
Now the Silence, Now the Peace 141
O God of Spring and Summer Days 106
Sorrow and Gladness 135
The House of Faith 108
This Is the Hour 154

Eucharist: see Lord's Supper
Evangelism: see Missions, Witness

Evening
Day Is Done 165
Forth in the Peace of Christ We Go 169
Lord, Bid Your Servant Go in Peace 170
O Gracious Light 163
O Light Whose Splendor 164

Faith
Lord, Make Us Servants 100, 101
O God in Whom All Life Begins 105
The House of Faith 108
We Have Come at Christ's Own Bidding 23

Faithfulness of God
(see also Assurance, Trust in God)
Give Thanks to the Lord 58
God Has Spoken by the Prophets 150
God Whose Love We Cannot Measure 84
In Deep Despair I Cry to You 59
My Soul Proclaims with Wonder 4
O God of Spring and Summer Days 106
O Jesus, I Have Promised 125
O Light Whose Splendor 164
The Lord My Pasture Shall Prepare 45

Family
Heirs Together of God's Grace 120
O Joseph 18
Of Women and of Women's Hopes 130
Onward, You Saints 89

Farewell
Upstairs? Downstairs? 168

Fear
Away with Our Fears 9
Come to Me, O Weary Traveler 66
Music and Incense 92
Rejoice in Christ Jesus 75
Sorrow and Gladness 135
Surely It Is God Who Saves Me 121, 123

Following Christ: see Christian Life

Forgiveness
(see also Confession of Sin)
Bread Is Blessed and Broken	157
Forgive Me, Father, I Confess	146
Help Us Accept Each Other	110
How Blessed Are Those	47
In Deep Despair I Cry to You	59
Into Our Loneliness	91
Music and Incense	92
Now the Silence, Now the Peace	141
O God Who Made Us in Your Likeness	90
Our God Forgives Us	50
Sovereign Maker of All Things	28
Sunday's Palms Are Wednesday's Ashes	25, 26
Vain Our Lives	145
With Sounds of Gentle Stillness	112

Freedom
The House of Faith	108

Funerals
Faithful Vigil Ended	160
Lord, Bid Your Servant Go in Peace	170
Now Have You Set Your Servant Free	171
O Gracious Light	163
Since You Have, Too, Encountered Grief	162
We Are the Music Angels Sing	161

Gifts
of God
O God in Whom All Life Begins	105
What Can I Ask in Your Name	107

for God
Give with Simplicity	113
What Can I Ask in Your Name	107

Good Friday: see Cross of Christ, Suffering of Christ

Grace
Guided by God's Holy Grace	129
Mercy Rises Like a Mountain	94
Sing, My Soul, His Wondrous Love	85
Sovereign Maker of All Things	28

Gratitude: see Thanksgiving & Gratitude

Guidance
(see also Illumination, Providence)
Blessed Be the God of Israel	5
Bush by the Fire Illumed	98
By Your Streams of Living Waters	61
Come, Let Us Raise a Joyful Sound	51
Come, My Way, My Truth, My Life	126
Christ Be Beside Me	114
Day by Day	123
Grant Us Wisdom to Perceive You	103
Guided by God's Holy Grace	129
In God I Trust	49
Into Our Loneliness	91
God of Unknown, Distant Worlds	77
Light of the Minds That Know Him	109
Lord, Glorify Yourself Today	118
Now Thank We All Our God	86
O God in Whom All Life Begins	105
O Jesus, I Have Promised	125
Since You Are Shepherd	44
Sing, My Soul, His Wondrous Love	85
Teach Us, Good Lord, to Serve	104
The Lord My Pasture Shall Prepare	45
This Day God Gives Me	413
We Are Not Our Own	80
With Sounds of Gentle Stillness	112

Harvest
(see also Thanksgiving & Gratitude)
Hope Is the Harrowing	93
Now the Silence, Now the Peace	141

Healing: see Sickness & Healing
Heaven: see New Heaven & Earth
Helper: see Refuge

Heritage
God Has Spoken by the Prophets	150
Heirs Together of God's Grace	120
Lord, Make Us Saints	102
Now Thank We All Our God	86
Onward, You Saints	89
We Are Not Our Own	80
We Praise You, God, for Women	82

Holiness: see Sanctification

Holy Spirit
Come Holy Spirit, Revive Your Church	40
Dove to Flesh	42
Holy Spirit, Truth Divine	41
To God with Gladness Sing	52

TOPICAL INDEX

Holy Week
Hosanna, Hosanna! 29
How Shallow Former Shadows Seem 33
O Lord, Eternal Light of God 19
Sunday's Palms Are Wednesday's Ashes 25, 26
Three Tall Trees Grew on a Windy Hill 32
What Are These Wounds 34

Hope
Away with Our Fears 9
Hope Is a Star 12
Hope Is the Harrowing 93
Isaiah the Prophet 2
When God's Time Had Ripened 8

Humility
Give With Simplicity 113
Sunday's Palms Are Wednesday's Ashes 25, 26
Vain Our Lives 145

Illumination
(see also Guidance, Light)
Come, Let Us Raise a Joyful Sound 51
Light of the Minds That Know Him 109
O Lord, Eternal Light of God 19

Immortality: see Eternal Life
Incarnation: see Christmas

Joy
Come, Let Us Raise a Joyful Sound 51
Come, My Way, My Truth, My Life 126
Hope Is a Star 12
Love Is of God 124
Music and Incense 92
Old Abraham Fell Down 78
Rejoice in Christ Jesus 75
When the Lord Restored Our Fortunes 57

Judge, God/Christ as
God's Judgment Comes Like Fire 133

Justice
(see also Society/Social Concerns)
Empty Is the Manger 137, 138
Isaiah the Prophet 2
May Peace Abide in Us 111
Of Women and of Women's Hopes 130
Our God Forgives Us 50
Praise the Living God Who Sings 88
We Are Not Our Own 80
When Broken Is Normal 136

Justification: see Forgiveness

King, God/Christ as
(see also Ascension)
Christ Be Beside Me 114
Christ the King, Enthroned in Splendor 39
Glory to Christ on High! 87
Isaiah the Prophet 2
Now Thank We All Our God 86
Praise Him As He Mounts the Skies 38
Rejoice, the Lord Is King! 134
Sing, My Soul, His Wondrous Love 85
We Marvel at Your Mighty Deeds 81
You Are a Priest Forever 55

Kingdom
Let Us Come Now to the Kingdom 142
Music and Incense 92
Rejoice, the Lord Is King! 134

Lamb of God
Glory to Christ on High! 87

Laments
(see also Afflictions)
As Panting Deer 48
In Deep Despair I Cry to You 59
O God, on Whom We Lost Our Hold 132

Law of God
Your Law, O Lord, Is Perfect 43

Lent
(see also Holy Week, Laments, Suffering of Christ)
Hosanna, Hosanna! 29
How Shallow Former Shadows Seem 33
Myrrh-Bearing Mary 67, 68
Sovereign Maker of All Things 28
Sunday's Palms Are Wednesday's Ashes 25, 26
Three Tall Trees Grew on a Windy Hill 32
What Are These Wounds 34

Liberty: see Freedom

Life of Christ
O Carpenter 24
O Lord, Eternal Light of God 19
Terra Sancta, Holy Land 99
Three Tall Trees Grew on a Windy Hill 32
When Jesus Entered Jericho 70
Woman in the Night 21, 22

TOPICAL INDEX

Light
Before the Earth Was Tossed in Space 76
Christ the King, Enthroned in Splendor 39
Day Is Done 165
God Has Spoken by the Prophets 150
How Shallow Former Shadows Seem 33
Light of the Minds That Know Him 109
Love Is of God 124
O Lord, Eternal Light of God 19
Town of David 13

Lord's Prayer
Father in Heaven 65
Our Father in Heaven 64

Lord's Supper
All Who Hunger, Gather Gladly 156
And As They Ate 155
Bread Is Blessed and Broken 157
Come in Holy Awe and Truth 152
Come, My Way, My Truth, My Life 126
Come, Satisfy Your Thirst 62
Draw Nigh and Take 158
Let Us Come Now to the Kingdom 142
Music and Incense 92
Taking Bread to Bless and Break 95
The Empty-Handed Fishermen 72
The Lord Is Here! 153
This Is the Hour 154
When Christians Shared Agape Meals 96
With the Body That Was Broken 31
Without the Fire 127

Lordship of Christ: see Ascension & Reign of Christ; King, God/Christ as

Love
  God's love to us
  As Panting Deer 48
  By Your Streams of Living Waters 61
  Come, My Way, My Truth, My Life 126
  Come, Satisfy Your Thirst 62
  Day Is Done 165
  Give Thanks to the Lord 58
  God of Unknown, Distant Worlds 77
  God Whose Love We Cannot Measure 84
  How Shallow Former Shadows Seem 33
  In Deep Despair I Cry to You 59
  Love Is of God 124
  Now Thank We All Our God 86
  Our God Forgives Us 50
  Since You Are Shepherd 44
  Sing, My Soul, His Wondrous Love 85
  The Empty-Handed Fishermen 72
  Where You Are, There Is Life 79
  of God
  Day by Day 123
  Give Thanks to the Lord 58
  Hope Is a Star 12
  If I Could Visit Bethlehem 14
  Light of the Minds That Know Him 109
  My Soul Proclaims with Wonder 4
  Not for Tongues of Heaven's Angels 73
  Sovereign Maker of All Things 28
  Teach Us, Good Lord, to Serve 104
  for others, neighbors
  Forth in the Peace of Christ We Go 169
  Give with Simplicity 113
  Heirs Together of God's Grace 120
  Help Us Accept Each Other 110
  Hope Is a Star 12
  Isaiah the Prophet 2
  Lord, Make Me an Alleluia 116, 117
  Lord, Make Us Servants 100, 101
  May Peace Abide in Us 111
  Sunday's Palms Are Wednesday's Ashes 25, 26
  Taking Bread to Bless and Break It 95
  We Are Not Our Own 80
  Were the World to End Tomorrow 115
  When Christians Shared Agape Meals 96

Majesty of God
God of Grace and God of Laughter 131
God of Unknown, Distant Worlds 77
O God, on Whom We Lost Our Hold 132
To God With Gladness Sing 52
We Marvel at Your Mighty Deeds 81
Who Is This King of Glory? 46
Wondrous God, More Named Than Known 128

Mercy
How Blessed Are Those 47
In God I Trust 49
Mercy Rises Like a Mountain 94
Sing, My Soul, His Wondrous Love 85
Sovereign Maker of All Things 28
Surely It Is God Who Saves Me 121, 122
Vain Our Lives 145

Ministry and Service
(see also Ordination)
Forth in the Peace of Christ We Go 169
Heirs Together of God's Grace 120
Lord, Make Us Saints 102
Lord, Make Us Servants 100, 101
Taking Bread to Bless and Break 95
Teach Us, Good Lord, to Serve 104
There a Friend Is Weeping 119
We Are Ambassadors for Christ 74
When Christians Shared Agape Meals 96
Woman in the Night 21, 22

Miracles
Bush by the Fire Illumed 98
Old Abraham Fell Down 78
Sing of God Made Manifest 17
The Empty-Handed Fishermen 72
They Have No Wine 71
When Lazarus Lay within the Tomb 37

Missions
Forth in the Peace of Christ We Go 169
Heirs Together of God's Grace 120
Lord, Glorify Yourself Today 118
Lord, Make Us Saints 102
Lord, Make Us Servants 100, 101
Onward, You Saints 89
Praise the Living God Who Sings 88
Taking Bread to Bless and Break 95
Teach Us, Good Lord, to Serve 104
There a Friend Is Weeping 119
We Are Ambassadors for Christ 74
We Are Not Our Own 80
Were the World to End Tomorrow 115
When Christians Shared Agape Meals 96

Morning
This Day God Gives Me 143

Music
God of Grace and God of Laughter 131
Music and Incense 92
On Angels' and Archangels' Wings 144
Praise the Living God Who Sings 88
Sing, My Soul, His Wondrous Love 85
The Lord Has Made Known His Salvation 53
To God with Gladness Sing 52
We Are the Music Angels Sing 161

New Heaven and Earth
Isaiah the Prophet 2
Let Us Come Now to the Kingdom 142
Mercy Rises Like a Mountain 94
Now the Silence, Now the Peace 141
Praise Him As He Mounts the Skies 38
Rejoice, the Lord Is King! 134
When Broken Is Normal 136

New Year—Old Year
Grey Ashes Fall 166
Now Greet the Swiftly Changing Year 167

Obedience
(see also Will of God)
O God Who Made Us in Your Likeness 90
Sovereign Maker of All Things 28
Sunday's Palms Are Wednesday's Ashes 25, 26

Offering
(see also Commitment & Dedication, Will of God)
Empty Is the Manger 137, 138
Give with Simplicity 113
King of Glory, King of Peace 83
Taking Bread to Bless and Break 95
We Are Not Our Own 80
What Can I Ask in Your Name 107

Opening of Worship
Come, Let Us Raise a Joyful Sound 51
Let Us Come Now to the Kingdom 142
Now the Silence, Now the Peace 141
On Angels' and Archangels' Wings 144
Onward, You Saints 89
The Empty-Handed Fishermen 72
This Day God Gives Me 143

Ordination: see Ministry & Service
Palm Sunday: see Holy Week

Parables
And Jesus Said 69

Patience
O God of Spring and Summer Days 106

TOPICAL INDEX

Peace
Inner
Holy Spirit, Truth Divine 41
Hope Is a Star 12
Love Is of God 124
May Peace Abide in Us 111
Mercy Rises Like a Mountain 94
O God of Spring and Summer Days 106
They Cast Their Nets in Galilee 63
To God With Gladness Sing 52
With Sounds of Gentle Stillness 112

World
A Babe Is Born 11
Hope Is a Star 12
Isaiah the Prophet 2
King of Glory, King of Peace 83
Lord, Make Us Servants 100, 101
May Peace Abide in Us 111
Mercy Rises Like a Mountain 94
O Child of Promise, Come! 1
Our God Forgives Us 50
Taking Bread to Bless and Break 95
Where You Are, There Is Life 79

Pentecost
Come Holy Spirit, Revive Your Church 40
Dove to Flesh 42
Holy Spirit, Truth Divine 41

Pilgrimage & Conflict
(see also Christian Life)
Day by Day 123
Now Thank We All Our God 86
O God in Whom All Life Begins 105
Terra Sancta, Holy Land 99
They Cast Their Nets in Galilee 63

Praise & Adoration
(see also Alleluias, Doxologies, Opening of Worship)
Come, Let Us Raise a Joyful Sound 51
Give Thanks to the Lord 58
Give with Simplicity 113
Glory to Christ on High! 87
God of Grace and God of Laughter 131
King of Glory, King of Peace 83
Lord, Make Me an Alleluia 116, 117
Now Thank We All Our God 86
O Gracious Light 163
On Angels' and Archangels' Wings 144
Praise Him As He Mounts the Skies 38
Praise the Living God Who Sings 88
Rejoice, Lord Is King! 134
Sing, My Soul, His Wondrous Love 85
Surely It Is God Who Saves Me 121, 122
To God with Gladness Sing 52
We Praise You, O God 82
When the Lord Restored Our Fortunes 57
Who Is This King of Glory? 46
Wondrous God, More Named Than Known 128

Prayer
Come, My Way, My Truth, My Life 126
Day by Day 123
Father in Heaven 65
Grant Us Wisdom to Perceive You 103
Lord, Make Me an Alleluia 116, 117
Now the Silence, Now the Peace 141
O God in Whom All Life Begins 105
Our Father in Heaven 64
What Can I Ask in Your Name 107

Preaching: see Word of God)

Presence, God's
Bread Is Blessed and Broken 157
Come, My Way, My Truth, My Life 126
Come, Satisfy Your Thirst 62
Grant Us Wisdom to Perceive You 103
In Deep Despair I Cry to You 59
In God I Trust 49
King of Glory, King of Peace 83
Lord, Glorify Yourself Today 118
Now the Silence, Now the Peace 141
O Jesus, I Have Promised 125
The Lord Is Here! 153
Where You Are, There Is Life 79
With Sounds of Gentle Stillness 112

Profession of Faith
(see also Commitment & Dedication)
Oh, I Believe That God 147
We Praise You, O God 82

Promises
(see also Covenant)
Blessed Be the God of Israel 5
Hope Is the Harrowing 93
O God in Whom All Life Begins 105

Protection: see Refuge

Providence
(see also Guidance)
The Empty-Handed Fishermen 72

Race & Culture: see Society/Social Concerns

Redemption
(see also Deliverance, Salvation)
Forgive Me, Father, I Confess 146
God Whose Love We Cannot Measure 84
Hope Is the Harrowing 93
Into Our Loneliness 91
Mercy Rises Like a Mountain 94
Music and Incense 92
O Carpenter 24
O Child of Promise, Come! 1
O God Who Made Us in Your Likeness 90
Send Forth Your Spirit, O Lord 54
Sorrow and Gladness 135
Sovereign Maker of All Things 28
Sunday's Palms Are Wednesday's Ashes 25, 26
Without the Fire 127

Reformation: see Heritage

Refuge
Guided by God's Holy Grace 129
O God of Spring and Summer Days 106
Sorrow and Gladness 135

Repentance: see Confession of Sin, Forgiveness

Responsibility
Give with Simplicity 113
God in His Love for Us 139
Grant Us Wisdom to Perceive You 103
O God Who Made Us in Your Likeness 90
There a Friend Is Weeping 119
We Are Not Our Own 80
We Who Preach a Church United 97
Were the World to End Tomorrow 115

Rest
Come to Me, O Weary Traveler 66

Resurrection: see Easter

Return of Christ
Before the Earth Was Tossed in Space 76
O Child of Promise, Come! 1

Salvation
(see also Deliverance, Redemption)
Come, My Way, My Truth, My Life 126
Draw Nigh and Take 158
Forgive Me, Father, I Confess 146
How Shallow Former Shadows Seem 33
Into Our Loneliness 91
Make Songs of Joy 36
O Carpenter 24
O Child of Promise, Come! 1
On This Day the Lord Has Acted 56
Sovereign Maker of All Things 28
Sunday's Palms Are Wednesday's Ashes 25, 26
Surely It Is God Who Saves Me 121, 122
The Babe in Beth'lem's Manger Laid 10
The Tomb Is Empty! 35
Town of David 13
When God's Time Had Ripened 8
When Jesus Entered Jericho 70
Without the Fire 127

Sanctification
Holy Spirit, Truth Divine 41
Into Our Loneliness 91
Sovereign Maker of All Things 28
Sunday's Palms Are Wednesday's Ashes 25, 26
Teach Us, Good Lord, to Serve 104
With Sounds of Gentle Stillness 112

Security: see Refuge
Service: see Ministry & Service

Shepherd, God/Christ as
And Jesus Said 69
As Panting Deer 48
By Your Streams of Living Waters 61
Since You Are Shepherd 44
The Lord My Pasture Shall Prepare 45

Sickness and Healing
Music and Incense 92
Sorrow and Gladness 135
There a Friend Is Weeping 119

Sin
(see also Confession of Sin, Forgiveness)
How Blessed Are Those 47
Into Our Loneliness 91
Vain Our Lives 145

TOPICAL INDEX

Society/Social Concerns
(see also Industry & Labor, Poverty, Stewardship)
All Who Hunger, Gather Gladly 156
Bush by the Fire Illumed 98
Empty Is the Manger 137, 138
Give with Simplicity 113
God Has Spoken by the Prophets 150
God in His Love for Us 139
Help Us Accept Each Other 110
Isaiah the Prophet 2
Mercy Rises Like a Mountain 94
O God, on Whom We Lost Our Hold 132
Praise the Living God Who Sings 88
Taking Bread to Bless and Break 95
We Are Not Our Own 80
We Praise You God, for Women 140
When Broken Is Normal 136
When Jesus Entered Jericho 70

Stewardship
Isaiah the Prophet 2
God in His Love for Us 139
O God Who Made Us in Your Likeness 90
When Jesus Entered Jericho 70

Suffering of Christ
(see also Cross of Christ, Lent)
Hosanna, Hosanna! 29
O Lord, Eternal Light of God 19
Three Tall Trees Grew on a Windy Hill 32

Temptation and Trial
(see also Afflictions)
As Panting Deer 48
Bush by the Fire Illumed 98
Come to Me, O Weary Traveler 66
God Whose Love We Cannot Measure 84
In Deep Despair I Cry to You 59
Into Our Loneliness 91
Music and Incense 92
O God, on Whom We Lost Our Hold 132
O Jesus, I Have Promised 125
Our God Forgives Us 50
Sorrow and Gladness 135
The Lord My Pasture Shall Prepare 45
They Cast Their Nets in Galilee 63
Vain Our Lives 145
When the Lord Restored Our Fortunes 57

Thanksgiving and Gratitude
Come, Let Us Raise a Joyful Sound 51
Give Thanks to the Lord 58
God Whose Love We Cannot Measure 84
Now Thank We All Our God 86
On This Day the Lord Has Acted 56
Our God Forgives Us 50
When the Lord Restored Our Fortunes 57

Transfiguration
Before the Earth Was Tossed in Space 76
Sing of God Made Manifest 17
We Have Come at Christ's Own Bidding 23

Trial: see Temptation & Trial

Trinity
Christ the King, Enthroned in Splendor 39
God Has Spoken by the Prophets 150
God Whose Love We Cannot Measure 84
Oh, I Believe That God 147
On Angels' and Archangels' Wings 144

Trust in God
My Soul Proclaims with Wonder 4
Now Thank We All Our God 86
O God of Spring and Summer Days 106
O Jesus, I Have Promised 125
Sing, My Soul, His Wondrous Love 85
Surely It Is God Who Saves Me 121, 122
Told of God's Favor 3

Unity
Come in Holy Awe and Truth 152
Heirs Together of God's Grace 120
Help Us Accept Each Other 110
Let Us Come Now to the Kingdom 142
Lord, Make Us Servants 100, 101
O God in Whom All Life Begins 105
Of Women and of Women's Hopes 130
Onward, You Saints 89
We Praise You, O God 82
We Who Preach a Church United 97

Victory
O God of Spring and Summer Days 106
The Lord Has Made Known His Salvation 53

Vocation: see Ministry & Service
Walk with God: see Christian Life

Warfare, Spiritual
In God I Trust 49
O Jesus, I Have Promised 125
They Cast Their Nets in Galilee 63
Who Is This King of Glory 46

Will of God
(see also Obedience)
O God Who Made Us in Your Likeness 90

Wisdom
Grant Us Wisdom to Perceive You 103

Witness
(see also Missions)
Away with Our Fears 9
Bush by the Fire Illumed 98
By Your Streams of Living Waters 61
Christ Be Beside Me 114
Empty Is the Manger 137, 138
Forth in the Peace of Christ We Go 169
Give with Simplicity 113
Heirs Together of God's Grace 120
Help Us Accept Each Other 110
If I Could Visit Bethlehem 14
Lord, Glorify Yourself Today 118
Lord, Make Me an Alleluia 116, 117
Lord, Make Us Saints 102
Lord, Make Us Servants 100, 101
May Peace Abide in Us 111
O God in Whom All Life Begins 105
O God Who Made Us in Your Likeness 90
O Joseph 18
Onward, You Saints 89
Praise the Living God Who Sings 88
Surely It Is God Who Saves Me 121, 122
Taking Bread to Bless and Break It 95
Teach Us, Good Lord, to Serve 104
There a Friend Is Weeping 119
Told of God's Favor 3
We Are Ambassadors for Christ 74
We Are Not Our Own 80
We Have Come at Christ's Own Bidding 23
We Who Preach a Church United 97
Were the World to End Tomorrow 115
What Can I Ask in Your Name 107
When Christians Shared Agape Meals 96
Woman in the Night 21, 22

Women/Women's Issues
And Jesus Said 69
Mary, Woman of the Promise 7
My Soul Proclaims with Wonder 4
Myrrh-Bearing Mary 67, 68
O God, on Whom We Lost Our Hold 132
Of Women and of Women's Hopes 130
Old Abraham Fell Down 78
Told of God's Favor 3
We Praise You God, for Women 140
Who Better Than Mary 20
Woman in the Night 21, 22
Wondrous God, More Named 128
Young Mary Lived in Nazareth 6

Word of God
By Your Streams of Living Waters 61
God Has Spoken by the Prophets 150
God's Judgment Comes Like Fire 133
The Word of God 149
Where You Are, There Is Life 79

Authors, translators, and sources of texts

Addison, Joseph (1672-1719)
    The Lord My Pasture Shall Prepare 45
Allen, James (1734-1804)
    Glory to Christ on High! 87
Apostles' Creed, The
    Oh, I Believe That God 147
Bangor Antiphoner (ca. 690)
    Draw Nigh and Take 158
Bartlett, Barbara B.
    Ol' Noah Got Mad 60
Bell, John (b. 1949)
    Bread Is Blessed and Broken 157
Benedict, St. (ca. 480-ca. 543)
    Grant Us Wisdom to Perceive You 103
Bode, John Ernest (1816-1874)
    O Jesus, I Have Promised 125
Bonar, Horatius (1808-1889)
    This Is the Hour 154
Boniface, St. (680-754)
    God Whose Love We Cannot Measure 84
Briggs, George Wallace (1875-1959)
    God Has Spoken by the Prophets 150
Brokering, Herbert (b. 1926)
    Guided by God's Holy Grace 129
    Mercy Rises Like a Mountain 94
Bush, AnnaMae Meyer (b. 1947)
    Heirs Together of God's Grace 120
Chesterton, Frances
    How Far Is It to Bethlehem? 15
Dalles, John A. (b. 1954)
    Vain Our Lives 145
Daw, Carl P., Jr. (b. 1944)
    As Panting Deer 48
    God of Grace and God of Laughter 131
    How Shallow Former Shadows Seem 33
    My Soul Proclaims with Wonder 4
    Now Have You Set Your Servant Free 171
    O God in Whom All Life Begins 105
    O God Who Made Us in Your Likeness 90
    O God, on Whom We Lost Our Hold 132
    O Light Whose Splendor 164
    Sing of God Made Manifest 17
    Sovereign Maker of All Things 28
    Surely It Is God Who Saves Me 121, 122
    The House of Faith 108
    We Have Come at Christ's Own Bidding 23
    We Marvel at Your Mighty Deeds 81
    When God's Time Had Ripened 8
    With the Body That Was Broken 31
    Wondrous God, More Named Than Known 128

Decker, Mark
    Our God Forgives Us 50
Duck, Ruth (b. 1947)
    We Praise You, God, for Women 140
Dudley-Smith, Timothy (b. 1926)
    Faithful Vigil Ended 160
    Light of the Minds That Know Him 109
    Not for Tongues of Heaven's Angels 73
    The Lord Is Here! 153
Dunstan, Sylvia (1955-1993)
    All Who Hunger, Gather Gladly 156
    Come to Me, O Weary Traveler 66
    The Tomb Is Empty 35
Edwards, Rusty (Howard M.) (b. 1955)
    Rejoice in Christ Jesus 75
Fleischaker, Mary Francis
    Mary, Woman of the Promise 7
Francis of Assisi, St. (1182-1226)
    Lord, Make Us Servants 100, 101
Green, Fred Pratt (b. 1903)
    God in His Love for Us 139
Gregory the Great (6th cent.)
    Now Let Us All with One Accord 30
Grindal, Gracia (b. 1943)
    A Babe Is Born 11
    And As They Ate 155
    And Jesus Said 69
    Come Holy Spirit, Revive Your Church 40
    Father in Heaven 65
    God's Judgment Comes Like Fire 133
    How Blessed Are Those 47
    Oh, I Believe That God 147
    Sorrow and Gladness 135
    We Praise You, O God 82
    When the Lord Restored Our Fortunes 57
Herbert, George (1593-1633)
    Come, My Way, My Truth, My Life 126
    King of Glory, King of Peace 83
Ignatius of Loyola, St. (1491-1556)
    Teach Us, Good Lord to Serve 104
Isaiah, First Song of
    Surely It Is God Who Saves Me 121, 122
Kaan, Fred (b. 1929)
    Help Us Accept Each Other 110
    Upstairs? Downstairs? 168
    Were the World to End Tomorrow 115
Kingo, Thomas H. (1634-1703)
    Sorrow and Gladness 135

AUTHORS, TRANSLATORS, AND SOURCES OF TEXTS

Landis, Keith (b. 1922)
    Come, Satisfy Your Thirst 62
    Lord, Glorify Yourself Today 118
    Our Father in Heaven 64
    Your Law, O Lord, Is Perfect 43

Leach, Richard (b.1953)
    Dove to Flesh 42
    Hope Is the Harrowing 93
    O Carpenter 24
    Old Abraham Fell Down and Laughed 78
    The Empty-Handed Fisherman 72
    Told of God's Favor 3
    When Broken Is Normal 136
    Where Was the Greater Struggle? 27

Longfellow, Samuel (1819-1892)
    Holy Spirit, Truth Divine 41

Lord's Prayer, The
    Father in Heaven 65
    Our Father in Heaven 64

Magnificat **(Song of Mary)**
    My Soul Proclaims with Wonder 4

Manasseh, Prayer of
    Sovereign Maker of All Things 28

Martinson, Joel (b.1960)
    We Are Ambassadors for Christ 74

Maule, Graham
    Bread Is Blessed and Broken 157

Miller, Jim (b. 1940)
    As a Child We Take This Bread 159

Murray, Shirley Erena (b. 1931)
    Of Women and of Women's Hopes 130

Nativity Hymns, 1745
    Away with Our Fears 9

Neale, John Mason (1818-1866)
    Draw Nigh and Take 158

Nunc Dimittis
    Faithful Vigil Ended 160
    Lord, Bid Your Servant Go in Peace 170
    Now Have You Set Your Servant Free 171

O'Brien, Maureen
    O Joseph 18

O'Driscoll, Herbert (b. 1928)
    Three Tall Trees Grew on a Windy Hill 32

Patterson, Joy F. (b. 1932)
    By Your Streams of Living Waters 61
    God of Unknown, Distant Worlds 77
    Hosanna, Hosanna! 29
    In Deep Despair I Cry to You 59
    Isaiah the Prophet 2
    When Lazarus Lay Within the Tomb 37

Percy, William Alexander (1885-1942)
    They Cast Their Nets in Galilee 63

Perry, Michael (b. 1942)
    God Whose Love We Cannot Measure 84

Phos Hilaron
    O Gracious Light 163
    O Light Whose Splendor 164

Quinn, James (b. 1919)
    Blessed Be the God of Israel 5
    Christ Be Beside Me 114
    Christ the King, Enthroned in Splendor 39
    Day Is Done 165
    Forth in the Peace of Christ We Go 169
    Lord, Bid Your Servant Go in Peace 170
    Lord, Make Us Servants 100, 101
    Love Is of God 124
    Now Let Us All with One Accord 30
    O Child of Promise, Come 1
    Praise Him As He Mounts the Skies 38
    This Day God Gives Me 143
    To God with Gladness Sing 52
    Town of David 13
    Word of God, Come Down on Earth 148

Richard of Chicester, St. (13th cent.)
    Day by Day 123

Rinkhart, Martin (1586-1649)
    Now Thank We All Our God 86

Robb, David A. (b. 1932)
    Lord Make Us Saints 102
    May Peace Abide in Us 111
    O Joseph 18
    O Lord, Eternal Light of God 19
    Praise the Living God Who Sings 88
    Since You Are Shepherd 44
    When Christians Shared Agape Meals 96
    With Sounds of Gentle Stillness 112

Rowthorn, Jeffery (b. 1934)
    Taking Bread to Bless and Break 95

Sedio, Mark (b. 1954)
    Come, Let Us Raise a Joyful Song 51
    Give Thanks to the Lord 58
    Onward, You Saints 89
    The Babe in Beth'lem's Manger Laid 10
    When Jesus Entered Jericho 70

Simeon, Song of
    Faithful Vigil Ended 160
    Lord, Bid Your Servant Go in Peace 170
    Now Have You Set Your Servant Free 171

Slovak
    Now Greet the Swiftly Changing Year 167

SPCK Psalms and Hymns, Appendix, 1869
    O Jesus, I Have Promised 125

Starke, Johann Friedrich
    Come in Holy Awe and Truth 152

AUTHORS, TRANSLATORS, AND SOURCES OF TEXTS

Te Deum Laudamus
We Praise You, O God 82
Thomas à Kempis (1380-1471)
Without the Fire 127
Tranousky, Jiri (17th cent.)
Make Songs of Joy 36
Troeger, Thomas H. (b. 1945)
The Word of God Was from the Start 149
Tucker, F. Bland (1895-1984)
O Gracious Light 163
Uehlein, Christopher (b. 1931)
May This Water Keep Us Aware 151
Vajda, Jaroslav J. (b. 1919)
Come in Holy Awe and Truth 152
Make Songs of Joy 36
Now Greet the Swiftly Changing Year 167
Now the Silence, Now the Peace 141
Where You Are, There Is Life 79
Wesley, Charles (1707-1788)
Away with Our Fears 9
Rejoice, the Lord Is King! 134
Whitney, Rae E. (b. 1927)
Before the Earth Was Tossed in Space 76
Empty Is the Manger 137, 138
Forgive Me, Father, I Confess 146
Give with Simplicity 113
Grant Us Wisdom to Perceive You 103
Grey Ashes Fall 166
Into Our Loneliness 91
Let Us Come Now to the Kingdom 142
Lord, Make Me an Alleluia 116, 117
Music and Incense 92
Myrrh-Bearing Mary 67, 68
O God of Spring and Summer Days 106
On Angels' and Archangels' Wings 144
Since You Have, Too, Encountered Grief .. 162
Sunday's Palms Are Wednesday's Ashes .. 25, 26
Teach Us, Good Lord, to Serve 104
Terra Sancta, Holy Land 99
That King before Whose Majesty 16
There a Friend Is Weeping 119
They Have No Wine 71
We Who Preach a Church United 97
What Are These Wounds 34
What Can I Ask in Your Name 107
Who Better Than Mary 20
Without the Fire 127
Young Mary Lived in Nazareth 6

Wold, Wayne L. (b. 1954)
Bush by the Fire Illumed 98
Wren, Brian (b. 1936)
Hope Is a Star 12
If I Could Visit Bethlehem 14
We Are Not Our Own 80
We Are the Music Angels Sing 161
Woman in the Night 21, 22
Zechariah, Song of
Blessed Be the God of Israel 5

Composers, Arrangers, and Sources of Music

Ahle, Johann R. (1625-1673)
    Liebster Jesu 148
American
    Land of Rest 170
    Noah's Ark 60
Arabic
    Arabia 45
Black, George
    Psalm 98 (The Lord Has Made Known) 53
    Psalm 104 (Send Forth Your Spirit) 54
    Psalm 118 (On This Day) 56
Busarow, Don (b. 1934)
    Ironwood 57
    St. Matthew the Younger 142
Bush, AnnaMae Meyer (b. 1947)
    Amanda 152
    Van Hamersveld 120
    Victory 36
Christian Lyre, 1830
    Pleading Savior 42
Cutts, Peter (b. 1937)
    Cherry Tree 43
    Hassman 104
    Many Mansions 114
    Minton 117
Darwall, John (1731-1789)
    Darwall's 148th 52
Doran, Carol (b. 1936)
    Benedict 103
    Kingo 135
Dykes, John B. (1823-1876)
    Melita 102
Edwards, Rusty (Howard M.) (b. 1955)
    Sadie 44
English
    Cherry Tree 43
    Cornish Carol 19
    Summer Court 144
English Country Songs, 1893
    Forest Green 5

Fedak, Alfred V. (b. 1953)
    Beach Haven 106
    Beach Spring 97
    Colfax 157
    Dance of Grace 28
    Davenport 72
    Day by Day 123
    Ecce, Deus 121
    Empty 138
    Gratia Plena 7
    Imago Dei, Cazenovia 90
    Kohelet 145
    Loveliness 91
    Myrrh-Bearing Mary 67
    New Disciples 21
    New World 136
    Peter's Brook 132
    Quinn 124
    Reitberg 161
    Rose of Bethlehem 8
    Sixth Night 167
    Three Tall Trees 32
    Upstairs, Downstairs 168
Good Old Songs, The
    Little Marlborough 1
Hackett, Kevin (b. 1956)
    Hobbs 130
Haynie, William S.
    Arabia 45
    Stable Room 15
Held, Wilbur (b. 1914)
    New Wine 71
    O Carpenter 24
    Sunday's Palms 26
    Town of David 13
Hesperian Harp, 1848
    Bourbon 30
Hill, Darcy (b. 1959)
    Sadie 44
Hillert, Richard (b. 1923)
    Teacher's Farewell 111
Hopp, Roy (b. 1951)
    Accord 105
    Arbor Day 115
    Bentbrook 81
    Isaac 131
    Oakdale 110
    Reinlyn 73
    Silver Creek 84
    Sister Bay 77, 128
    Turnberry 17

Hopson, Hal H. (b. 1933)
Corning 27
Nolan 86
Hurd, David (b. 1950)
Cyprian 163
Nexus 80
Surely It Is God 122
Husberg, Amanda
Here Am I 119
Mikhael Gideon Jacob 34
Johnson, David N. (1922-1987)
Sawyer's Exit 47
Summer Court 144
Joseph, Georg (d. 1668)
Angelus 169
Landis, Keith (b. 1922)
Cavanaugh 109
Colfax 157
Day by Day 123
Graham 153
Latimer 39
Midnight Cry 134
Pattison 64
Lovelace, Austin C. (b. 1919)
Embers 166
Samanthra 2
Martinson, Joel (b. 1960)
Anchorage 74
Bruern Abbey 154
Hillcrest 76
Joyful Steps 99
Kessler Park 41, 126
McAllister, Louise (1913-1960)
Bourbon 30
Mealy, Margaret (b. 1922)
Complainer 112
Holy Manna 61
Morris, Sally Ann (b. 1952)
Firm Anchor 150
Music, David W. (b. 1949)
Ballad of Mary 6
Nestor, Leo (b. 1948)
Carlton Way 95
Psalm 24 (Who Is This King) 46
Psalm 55 (In God I Trust) 49
Psalm 110 55
William 160
Original Sacred Harp, The, 1911
Teacher's Farewell 111

Patterson, Joy F. (b. 1932)
And Jesus Said 69
Duane 29
Hildegard of Bingen 140
Pavlechko, Thomas
Hellmers 159
Pelz, Walter L. (b. 1926)
God's Love 94
Wichita 129
Prins, Iteke (b. 1937)
Faith 108
Pulkingham, Betty (b. 1928)
East End 25
Fisherfolk 63
Holy Seed 162
Rickard, Jeffrey (b. 1942)
Cavanaugh 109
Cornish Carol 19
Graham 153
Kelvingrove 62
Latimer 39
Midnight Cry 134
Rowan, William P. (b. 1951)
Austin 66
Cardinal 33
Carpenter 18
Hunt 4
Seymour 12
Simmons 14
Smith 88
Timothy Square 96
Verbum Dei 149
Wicklund 22
Rutter, John (b. 1945)
Pattison 64
Sacred Harp, The, 1844
Beach Spring 97
Sawyer's Exit 47
Schulz-Widmar, Russell (b. 1944)
Bordy 3
Land of Rest 170
Sanjeev 143
Scott, K. Lee (b. 1950)
Young 101
Scottish
Kelvingrove 62

Sedio, Mark (b. 1954)
- Ause 10
- Chapel of the Incarnation 82
- Credo 147
- Enduring Love 58
- Father in Heaven 65
- God's Love 89
- Joyful Song 51
- Lowen 50
- New Wine 155
- Orava 79
- Zacchaeus 70

Sixteen Tune Settings, 1812
- Morning Song 59

Southern Harmony, The, 1835
- Complainer 112
- Holy Manna 61
- Prospect 16, 118
- Samanthra 2

Uehlein, Christopher (b. 1931)
- Cordell 151
- Wesely 87

Urwin, Ray W. (b. 1950)
- Alleluia Me Face 116
- Fenton 38
- Kidder 92

Vaughan Williams, Ralph (1872-1958)
- Forest Green 5
- Pleading Savior 42

Walker, David Charles (b. 1938)
- General Seminary 83

Welsh
- Ar Hyd y Nos 165

White, David Ashley (b. 1944)
- Austin 40
- Brewer 23
- Conway 127
- Denson 156
- Homage 125
- Josephine 85
- Julian of Norwich 139
- Kennan New 93
- Morning Song 59
- Nashua 133
- Nunc Dimittis 171
- Palmer Church 158
- Phos Hilaron 164
- Rochester 100
- Sheridan 146
- Simms 141
- St. Mark's Chapel 31
- Sumter 37
- Ward 48
- Winston 35

White, Jack Noble (b. 1938)
- Little Marlborough 1
- Prospect 16, 118

Wold, Wayne L. (b. 1954)
- Blarson 11
- Laughter 78
- Paramount 98
- True Peace 75

Wyton, Alec (b. 1921)
- Glory 107
- Hearts of Love 137
- Rejoice 68
- Ridgefield 20
- Whitney 113

Young, Carlton R. (b. 1924)
- Robert 9

Metrical Index

SM (Short meter: 66 86)
- Little Marlborough 1
- Teacher's Farewell 111

CM (Common meter: 86 86)
- Anchorage 74
- Faith 108
- Fisherfolk 63
- Graham 153
- Holy Seed 162
- Joyful Song 51
- Land of Rest 170
- Nashua 133
- O Carpenter 24
- Sadie 44
- Simmons 14
- Sumter 37
- Winston 35

CM with refrain
- Ause 10

CMD (Common Meter Double: 86 86 86 86)
- Accord 105
- Ballad of Mary 6
- Beach Haven 106
- Blarson 11
- Cardinal 33
- Forest Green 5
- Peter's Brook 132

LM (Long Meter: 88 88)
- Angelus 169
- Bourbon 30
- Cornish Carol 19
- Cyprian 163
- Davenport 72
- Hillcrest 76
- Laughter 78
- Prospect 16, 118
- Rochester 100
- Sheridan 146
- Summer Court 144
- Verbum Dei 149
- Young 101

555 4 D
- Kidder 92
- Many Mansions 114
- Sanjeev 143

55 55 with refrain
- Wicklund 22

55 55 D with refrain
- New Disciples 21

55 56 55
- Robert 9

65 63
- Colfax 157

65 64 D
- Loveliness 91

65 65 with refrain
- Here Am I 119

65 65 D
- Empty 138
- Hearts of Love 137
- Rose of Bethlehem 8
- William 160

656 846
- True Peace 75

664 666 4
- Wesely 87

66 64 D
- Paramount 98

666 4 D
- Whitney 113

66 66 66
- Hassman 104

66 66 88
- Darwall's 148th 52
- Midnight Cry 134

666 88 64
- Orava 79

67 67 66 66
- Nolan 86

68 68 86 7
- Credo 147

687 66
- Kennan New 93

74 74
- Stable Room 15

74 74 D
- Fenton 38
- General Seminary 83

76 76
- Cherry Tree 43

76 76 D
- Cavanaugh 109
- Complainer 112
- Corning 27
- Homage 125
- New Wine 71
- Oakdale 110

76 76 D with refrain
- Hunt 4

76 86 86 86
- Hildegard of Bingen 140

77 55 8
- Glory 107

77 77
- Hellmers 159
- Josephine 85
- Kessler Park 41, 126
- Upstairs, Downstairs 168

77 77 77
- Joyful Steps 99
- Sister Bay 77, 128
- Wichita 129

77 77 77 with Alleluias
- Smith 88

77 77 D
- Dance of Grace 28
- Turnberry 17

78 78 77
- Amanda 152

78 78 88
- Liebster Jesu 148

83 46
- Reitberg 161

84 84
- Victory 36

84 84 88 84
- Ar Hyd y Nos 165

86 86 6
- Timothy Square 96

86 86 86
- Bentbrook 81
- Morning Song 59

86 96 86
- Austin 40

METRICAL INDEX

87 87
- Arbor Day 115
- Austin 66
- Carpenter 18
- Cordell 151
- Gratia Plena 7
- Town of David 13

87 87 6
- Reinlyn 73

87 87 77
- God's Love 94
- Latimer 39

87 87 87
- Carlton Way 95
- St. Mark's Chapel 31

87 87 D
- Beach Spring 97
- Brewer 23
- Denson 156
- East End 25
- Ecce, Deus 121
- Firm Anchor 150
- Holy Manna 61
- Isaac 131
- Kohelet 145
- Pleading Savior 42
- Silver Creek 84
- St. Matthew the Younger 142
- Sunday's Palms 26
- Surely It Is God 122

88 84
- Minton 117
- Alleluia Me Face 116

88 86
- Benedict 103
- Embers 166
- Sixth Night 167

88 88 88
- And Jesus Said 69
- Arabia 45
- Melita 102

89 85
- Nexus 80

8 10 8
- New Wine 155

97 97
- Enduring Love 58

98 98
- Phos Hilaron 164

98 98 with refrain
- Imago Dei, Cazenovia 90

98 98 D
- Sawyer's Exit 47

99 99
- Conway 127

10 7 10 7
- Mikhael Gideon Jacob 34

10 8 7 8
- Lowen 50

10 9 10 9
- Bordy 3

10 10
- Palmer Church 158
- Quinn 124

10 10 10 10
- Bruern Abbey 154
- Hobbs 130
- Myrrh-Bearing Mary 67
- Rejoice 68
- Ward 48

10 10 10 10 10 10
- Nunc Dimittis 171

11 10 11 10
- God's Love 89
- Julian of Norwich 139

11 10 11 10 44 10
- Kingo 135

11 10 12 10
- Kelvingrove 62

11 11 11 11
- New World 136
- Pattison 64

12 7 11 8
- Father in Heaven 65

12 9 12 9
- Noah's Ark 60

12 11 11 9
- Ridgefield 20

12 12 13 13
- Duane 29

PM (Peculiar Meter)
- Chapel of the Incarnation 82

Irregular
- Day by Day 123
- Ironwood 57
- Samantha 2
- Seymour 12
- Simms 141
- Three Tall Trees 32
- Van Hamersveld 120
- Zacchaeus 70

Tune Names

Tune	Page
Accord	105
Alleluia Me Face	116
Amanda	152
Anchorage	74
And Jesus Said	69
Angelus	169
Ar Hyd y Nos	165
Arabia	45
Arbor Day	115
Ause	10
Austin (Rowan)	66
Austin (White)	40
Ballad of Mary	6
Beach Haven	106
Beach Spring	97
Benedict	103
Bentbrook	81
Blarson	11
Bordy	3
Bourbon	30
Brewer	23
Bruern Abbey	154
Cardinal	33
Carlton Way	95
Carpenter	18
Cavanaugh	109
Chapel of the Incarnation	82
Cherry Tree	43
Colfax	157
Complainer	112
Conway	127
Cordell	151
Corning	27
Cornish Carol	19
Credo	147
Cyprian	163
Dance of Grace	28
Darwall's 148th	52
Davenport	72
Day by Day	123
Denson	156
Duane	29
East End	25
Ecce, Deus	121
Embers	166
Empty	138
Enduring Love	58
Faith	108
Father in Heaven	65
Fenton	38
Firm Anchor	150
Fisherfolk	63
Forest Green	5
General Seminary	83
Glory	107
God's Love (Sedio)	89
God's Love (Pelz)	94
Graham	153
Gratia Plena	7
Hassman	104
Hearts of Love	137
Hellmers	159
Here Am I	119
Hildegard of Bingen	140
Hillcrest	76
Hobbs	130
Holy Manna	61
Holy Seed	162
Homage	125
Hunt	4
Imago Dei, Cazenovia	90
Ironwood	57
Isaac	131
Josephine	85
Joyful Song	51
Joyful Steps	99
Julian of Norwich	139
Kelvingrove	62
Kennan New	93
Kessler Park	41, 126
Kidder	92
Kingo	135
Kohelet	145
Land of Rest	170
Latimer	39
Laughter	78
Liebster Jesu	148
Little Marlborough	1
Loveliness	91
Lowen	50
Many Mansions	114
Melita	102
Midnight Cry	134
Mikhael Gideon Jacob	34
Minton	117
Morning Song	59
Myrrh-Bearing Mary	67
Nashua	133
New Disciples	21
New Wine (Held)	71
New Wine (Sedio)	155
New World	136
Nexus	80
Noah's Ark	60
Nolan	86
Nunc Dimittis	171
O Carpenter	24
Oakdale	110
Orava	79
Palmer Church	158
Paramount	98
Pattison	64
Peter's Brook	132
Phos Hilaron	164
Pleading Savior	42
Prospect	16, 118
Quinn	124
Reinlyn	73
Reitberg	161
Rejoice	68
Ridgefield	20
Robert	9
Rochester	100
Rose of Bethlehem	8
Sadie	44
Samantha	2
Sanjeev	143
Sawyer's Exit	47
Seymour	12
Sheridan	146
Silver Creek	84
Simmons	14
Simms	141
Sister Bay	77, 128
Sixth Night	167
Smith	88
St. Mark's Chapel	31
St. Matthew the Younger	142
Stable Room	15
Summer Court	144
Sumter	37
Sunday's Palms	26
Surely It Is God	122
Teacher's Farewell	111
Three Tall Trees	32
Timothy Square	96
Town of David	13
True Peace	75
Turnberry	17
Upstairs, Downstairs	168
Van Hamersveld	120
Verbum Dei	149
Victory	36
Ward	48
Wesely	87
Whitney	113
Wichita	129
Wicklund	22
William	160
Winston	35
Young	101
Zacchaeus	70

First Lines and Titles 223

Titles or refrains by which hymns may also be known are italicized

A Babe Is Born	11
All Who Hunger, Gather Gladly	156
And As They Ate	155
And Jesus Said	69
As a Child We Take This Bread	159
As Panting Deer	48
Away with Our Fears	9
Before the Earth Was Tossed in Space	76
Blessed Be the God of Israel	5
Bread Is Blessed and Broken	157
Bush by the Fire Illumed	98
By Your Streams of Living Waters	61
Christ Be Beside Me	114
Christ the King, Enthroned in Splendor	39
Come and Join the Song	21, 22
Come Holy Spirit, Revive Your Church	40
Come in Holy Awe and Truth	152
Come, My Way, My Truth, My Life	126
Come to Me, O Weary Traveler	66
Come, Let Us Raise a Joyful Sound	51
Come, Satisfy Your Thirst	62
Day by Day	123
Day Is Done	165
Didn't It Rain	60
Dove to Flesh	42
Draw Nigh and Take	158
Easter Hymn	35
Ecce, Deus	121, 122
Empty Is the Manger	137, 138
Faithful Vigil Ended	160
Father in Heaven	65
Forgive Me, Father, I Confess	146
Forth in the Peace of Christ We Go	169
Give Thanks to the Lord	58
Give with Simplicity	113
Glory to Christ on High!	87
God Has Spoken by the Prophets	150
God in His Love for Us	139
God of Grace and God of Laughter	131
God of Unknown, Distant Worlds	77
God Whose Love We Cannot Measure	84
God's Judgment Comes Like Fire	133
Grant Us Wisdom to Perceive You	103
Grey Ashes Fall	166
Guided by God's Holy Grace	129
Have Mercy on Me	49
Heirs Together of God's Grace	120
Help Us Accept Each Other	110
Here Am I	119
Holy Spirit, Truth Divine	41
Hope Is a Star	12
Hope Is the Harrowing	93
Hosanna, Hosanna!	29
How Blessed Are Those	47
How Far Is It to Bethlehem?	15
How Shallow Former Shadows Seem	33
If I Could Visit Bethlehem	14
In Deep Despair I Cry to You	59
In God I Trust	49
Into Our Loneliness	91
Isaiah the Prophet	2
King of Glory, King of Peace	83
Kyrie Pantokrator	28
Let Us Come Now to the Kingdom	142
Lift Up Your Heart!	134
Light of the Minds That Know Him	109
Lord Make Us Saints	102
Lord, Bid Your Servant Go in Peace	170
Lord, Glorify Yourself Today	118
Lord, Make Me an Alleluia	116, 117
Lord, Make Us Servants	100, 101
Love Is of God	124
Magnificat	4
Make Songs of Joy	36
Make Your Church, O Lord	95
Mary, Woman of the Promise	7
May Love Be Ours, O Lord	73
May Peace Abide in Us	111
May This Water Keep Us Aware	151
Mercy Rises Like a Mountain	94
Music and Incense	92
My Soul Proclaims with Wonder	4
Myrrh-Bearing Mary	67, 68
Not for Tongues of Heaven's Angels	73
Now Greet the Swiftly Changing Year	167
Now Have You Set Your Servant Free	171
Now Let Us All with One Accord	30
Now Thank We All Our God	86
Now the Silence, Now the Peace	141
Nowell, Nowell	10
Nunc Dimittis	160, 170, 171
O Carpenter	24
O Child of Promise, Come!	1
O Gates, Lift Up Your Heads	46
O God in Whom All Life Begins	105
O God of Spring and Summer Days	106
O God Who Made Us in Your Likeness	90
O God, on Whom We Lost Our Hold	132
O Gracious Light	163
O Jesus, I Have Promised	125
O Joseph	18
O Light Whose Splendor	164
O Lord, Eternal Light of God	19
O Lord, How Manifold Are Your Works	54
Of Women and of Women's Hopes	130
Oh, I Believe That God	147

FIRST LINES AND TITLES

Ol' Noah Got Mad 60
Old Abraham Fell Down 78
On Angels' and Archangels' Wings 144
On This Day the Lord Has Acted 56
Onward, You Saints 89
Our Father in Heaven 64
Our God Forgives Us 50
Phos Hilaron 164
Praise Him As He Mounts the Skies 38
Praise the Living God Who Sings 88
Praise (II) 83
Prayer of Manasseh 28
Psalm 19 43
Psalm 23 .... 44, 45
Psalm 24 46
Psalm 32 47
Psalm 42 48
Psalm 55 49
Psalm 85 50
Psalm 95 .... 51, 52
Psalm 98 53
Psalm 104 54
Psalm 110 55
Psalm 118 56
Psalm 126 57
Psalm 130 59
Psalm 136 58
Rejoice in Christ Jesus 75
Rejoice, the Lord Is King! 134
Restore in Us Your Image 90
Send Forth Your Spirit, O Lord 54
Since You Are Shepherd 44
Since You Have, Too, Encountered Grief 162
Sing of God Made Manifest 17
Sing, My Soul, His Wondrous Love 85
Sing to the Lord a New Song 53
Song of Mary 4
Song of Simeon 160, 170, 171
Song of Zechariah 5
Sorrow and Gladness 135
Sovereign Maker of All Things 28
Saint Mary the Virgin Said 20
Sunday's Palms Are Wednesday's Ashes 25, 26
Surely It Is God Who Saves Me 121, 122
Taking Bread to Bless and Break 95
Taste and See 156
Teach Us, Good Lord, to Serve 104
Te Deum Laudamus 82
Terra Sancta, Holy Land 99
That King before Whose Majesty 16
The Babe in Beth'lem's Manger Laid 10
The Call 126
The Empty-Handed Fishermen 72
The House of Faith 108
The Lord Has Made Known His Salvation 53
The Lord Is Here! 153
The Lord Is My Strength and My Song 56
The Lord My Pasture Shall Prepare 45
The Lord's Prayer 64, 65
The Lord's Revelation 55
The Tomb Is Empty! 35
The Word of God Was from the Start 149
There a Friend Is Weeping 119
These Are the Wounds 34
They Cast Their Nets in Galilee 63
They Have No Wine 71
This Day God Gives Me 143
This Is the Hour 154
Three Tall Trees Grew on a Windy Hill 32
To God with Gladness Sing 52
To Me Has God Shown Favor 4
Told of God's Favor 3
Town of David 13
Upstairs? Downstairs? 168
Vain Our Lives 145
We Are Ambassadors for Christ 74
We Are Not Our Own 80
We Are the Music Angels Sing 161
We Have Come at Christ's Own Bidding 23
We Marvel at Your Mighty Deeds 81
We Praise You, God, for Women 140
We Praise You, O God 82
We Who Preach a Church United 97
Were the World to End Tomorrow 115
What Are These Wounds 34
What Can I Ask in Your Name 107
When Broken Is Normal 136
When Christians Shared Agape Meals 96
When God Is a Child 12
When God's Time Had Ripened 8
When Jesus Entered Jericho 70
When Lazarus Lay within the Tomb 37
When the Lord Restored Our Fortunes 57
Where Was the Greater Struggle? 27
Where You Are, There Is Life 79
Who Better Than Mary 20
Who Is This King of Glory? 4
With Sounds of Gentle Stillness ....
With the Body That Was Broken ....
Without the Fire ....
Woman in the Night 21
Wondrous God, More Named Than Known 1
Word of God, Come Down on Earth 14
You Are a Priest Forever 5
Young Mary Lived in Nazareth ....
Your Law, O Lord, Is Perfect 43